ANIMAL WAYSHOWERS

The Lightworkers Ushering In 5D Consciousness

Tammy Billups

Bear & Company
Rochester, Vermont

Bear & Company
One Park Street
Rochester, Vermont 05767
www.BearandCompanyBooks.com

Bear & Company is a division of Inner Traditions International

Cataloging-in-Publication Data for this title is available from the Library of Congress

ISBN 978-1-59143-443-6 (print)
ISBN 978-1-59143-444-3 (ebook)

Printed and bound in the United States by Versa Press, Inc.

10 9 8 7 6 5 4 3 2 1

Text design and layout by Kenleigh Manseau
This book was typeset in Garamond Premier Pro with Fnord used as display typeface

To send correspondence to the author of this book, mail a first-class letter to the author c/o Inner Traditions • Bear & Company, One Park Street, Rochester, VT 05767, and we will forward the communication, or contact the author directly at **tammybillups.com**.

For the courageous wayshowers and lightworkers
unearthing a gentler, more loving way of being to
ease the journeys of all those in their wake.

✴

My beloved animal companions,
Bodhi and Rumi

Contents

FOREWORD

The Bodhisattva Hearts of Our Animal Kin

Linda Star Wolf, Ph.D.

For many years I have had a small plaque on my front porch that says, "Lord please help me to be the person that my dog believes I am." As whimsical as that statement is, it is also so very true. It is often said that our animal companions are the real masters of unconditional love and forgiveness.

During these tumultuous and shamanic times on our beautiful Mother Earth, many humans are opening up and gaining a deeper understanding that nothing comes into our lives by accident. If this is the case then everything that touches us is "on purpose." Once we drop into this deeper way of knowing and experiencing life, we can take a deep breath, let go, and trust life's journey with an open heart and mind.

Our animal relationships are "on purpose" as well, and never has it been more evident than when reading Tammy Billups newest book, *Animal Wayshowers*. This amazing author and spiritual healer of animals and people has documented the sage teachings of our animal companions and imparts that they are here to guide us into fifth-dimensional living. Tammy explains in the book that "animals are the ambassadors of 5D consciousness," and I couldn't agree more!

Tammy is a pioneer on the animal-human sacred soul partnership, and her transformational work over the last two decades has shed much light on the deeper reasons why we are with specific animals in our lives and how our souls orchestrate each step of our relationship for our mutual growth. Her wisdom touches me and resonates very much with my own experiences on my shamanic spiritual path.

Much like Tammy, I have always shared a deep love connection with all animals and oftentimes sought them out when I needed to feel accepted and loved unconditionally. In all honesty, I have remained a bit of a wild child and have often preferred the company of nature and my animal companions over humans.

Many years ago, my beloved Seneca Wolf Clan Grandmother, Twylah Nitsch, guided me into forming an even deeper connection to guidance and support from the "Creature Teachers" when I sought her out as a "medicine teacher." The sacred teaching is that animals both in physical form as well as in the spirit world are here to help humanity evolve through the transformations and initiations that we all go through. They are older than humans in their origins and carry a deeper wisdom. So contrary to the thought that humans are at the top and animals, plants, and minerals are lesser beings, it is quite the opposite.

This is not a new concept to the original peoples as they believed that we are all "family" and all beings are our brothers and sisters. This was not new to me since many of my childhood days were often spent visiting my grandfather and grandmother on their farm, along with the menagerie of chickens, rabbits, dogs, cats, hamsters, turtles, frogs, fish, and birds. Many years later in reflection, I realized my maternal grandmother, who was also a great animal lover, helped to ground and connect my sensitive nature to this Earth through the creatures I shared a love bond with. My early healing experiences being barefoot outside in nature with animals have remained an essential part of being on the shamanic medicine path that I am committed to walking daily.

Presently my husband and I live at our Loveland home surrounded by lush green forests and magical blue mountains in western North Carolina. Our animal family consists of three dogs, Koda, Mystic, and Anubis; one cat, Princess Lakshmi; two goats, Krishna and Pan; and a collection of hens and roosters, along with daily visits on our deck from squirrels, hummingbirds, wild birds, lizards, dragonflies, butterflies, bees, spiders, and lots of interesting insects and creatures. We are endlessly entertained, educated, and loved by all these magnificent wayshowers. These creature teachers seem to always show up at the exact moment that our hearts and spirits are open to receive their help and "medicine."

Over the years I have had many magical and meaningful encounters with wild animals in nature as well as those I have shared hearth and home with. In all their magnificent forms, they have all been teachers and guides. My beautiful Vision Wolf, who Tammy writes about in this book, was and still is the most amazing animal wayshower I have ever been blessed to encounter on any level. I, and many others who knew him, have said "there will never be another Vision Wolf." Belle was Vision's sweet momma and was a stray that, as fate would have it, found her way into the hearts and home of Salle and James

Redfield. I had met the Redfields in Sedona the year before at a spiritual conference where we were both teaching and we had formed a friendship, so I had heard about Belle's timely arrival into their lives and the imminent birth of puppies.

The synchronistic manner of how Vision Wolf came into my life as a puppy who almost didn't survive his birth process mirrored my own difficult birth process. I had no intention to bring a dog into my life at that moment while going through the complete dissolution of my old life on every level. I remember saying to Salle over the phone, "There is no way I can have a dog right now. I am way too busy with travel and workshops and dismantling my old life."

Spirit definitely had other plans! I had no idea how much I needed not just any dog, but this extraordinary "wolf dog" in my life. I cannot imagine having lived seventeen years through all the most pivotal decisions and transformations that radically changed the course of my life forever without Vision by my side every step of the way. He still visits me in my dreams and I can always sense when his frequency is reaching out to me from the Great Beyond. Because our bond is eternal and we have been together many times and in many other forms, I easily recognize the imprint of his soul's essence and am deeply blessed to have such a loving and wise guide who continues to assist me on my path.

So much wisdom can be ignited and many blessings received when we are able to humbly open our hearts and minds to create a deeper relationship with these higher beings of unconditional love who have seemingly synchronistically appeared in our lives at the perfect time, even when it doesn't feel perfect.

This wonderful book will take you on an openhearted

journey through the multidimensional relationship you share with *your* incredible animal companions and show you the way to embrace the 5D way of living that your animals are beautifully emulating for you.

Tammy Billups is a master teacher who shares much-needed guidance for animal lovers on the spiritual path, along with many deep, poignant, and powerful example stories of animal wayshowers that are sure to open your heart and have you looking at your animals with an even deeper reverence for all they are doing on your behalf. These magnificent beings have shown up right on time to offer us humans support on our way home, to guide by example how to be better multidimensional human beings as we learn how to embody love, wisdom, compassion, and forgiveness for ourselves and the world . . . especially now.

Thank you, Tammy, for being a wise, kindhearted two-legged with the good sense to follow your own heart and share these invaluable teachings from the animal lightworkers both here and in spirit who have crossed your path during their brief visit here on Earth.

LINDA STAR WOLF, PH.D., is the founding director and president of Venus Rising Association for Transformation and Venus Rising University. The creator of the Shamanic Breathwork process, she has led countless workshops and certified hundreds of Shamanic Breathwork facilitators around the world. She is the author of several books, including *Soul Whispering* and *Shamanic Breathwork: the Nature of Change.* Star Wolf lives in western North Carolina.

INTRODUCTION
Your Ascension Guides

Can you imagine your life without ever having shared your heart and home with animals? Millions of people have been transformed by the love of an animal, and I am no exception. Animals have had a monumental impact on my life. Like endless others, the first time I felt the purity and bliss of unconditional love was from an animal. In my twenties a cute little calico kitten looked into my soul and whispered *I see you, I love you,* and I was forever changed.

When that same kitty got her wings twelve years later, I was suddenly and quite unexpectedly able to see and feel her soul around me, going about her normal routine in the house. This experience catapulted me into a new level of awareness and fascination for learning more about the many dimensions that I suddenly had access to. It also initiated a challenging and transformational year that rocked me at my core and kicked my previous beliefs to the curb. It was a difficult period of time filled with loss and deep emotional pain, but through the darkest of nights, and there were many, it was my animal companions that stood in the fire with me. And they made it look so effortless.

I often wonder what our planet would be like if the animal kingdom wasn't holding the high watch for us humans to heal, grow, and evolve. Their presence in our lives is far more impactful and important for our emotional, physical, and spiritual growth than most will ever realize. Our animal companions are guiding lights that have been *showing us the way* to our hearts since the dawn of time. They offer portals into our soul for a deeper and more intimate understanding of the divine spark held in the sacred center of our being.

I am always in awe to learn, time and time again, that animals are the ones that can get through to people, rock them at their spiritual core, and break the chains that bind their hearts. The spiritual work they do on our behalf never ceases to amaze me. Throughout the last twenty-two years of working with animals and people through my holistic healing practice, I have often been overcome by the sheer strength, determination, courage, and endless love that animals tirelessly exude in their mission to support and awaken us. And much of the time, their purposeful efforts go unnoticed.

Our beloved animal companions are literally on the front lines of the animal kingdom's efforts to open our hearts and usher in 5D consciousness. In the pages ahead you will learn about the multitude of ways animals have taken on the role of ambassadors to raise the vibration of the planet to one filled with harmony and equality. You see, they have undercover spiritual missions rooted in helping you to navigate through the twists and turns of earthly life to expedite your ascension process to the land of ease and grace in the fifth dimension.

The motivation to write *Animal Wayshowers* originated from witnessing countless lightworker and wayshower animals consistently standing with their people, and many others, in the throes of 3D polarity to raise the collective consciousness. The extent of their service needs to be shared so people can be aware of the depth of their efforts on our behalf. This book not only illustrates how and why animals are bringing in a higher level of consciousness, it also provides tangible tools for you to join them in unearthing a new time on our planet.

Woven throughout the book, I share examples of extraordinary animals from around the world that have shown up for humanity in ways large and small. The people in the example stories are equally amazing, and I honor their courage to say *yes* to sharing intimate details of their "animal love story." I worked closely with them to ensure that every word has factual integrity. These true-life examples will help you to identify the ways your animal companions might be steering you in a direction that's significant for your growth and evolution.

With each and every example, I called in the animals' Higher Self (their soul) to join me so I could ensure their purposeful mission and teachings were relayed through the words. I invite you to connect with their wonderful energy to enhance your reading experience and receive the gift their story has for you. Their soul will undoubtedly be filled with joy and gratitude to serve you in this way.

In Part I, "Their Sacred Purpose," you will learn about the dynamics of an animal wayshower and how the soul contracts you share with your companions reveal themselves in 3D, 4D, and 5D. We dive into soul groups, streams of animal species consciousness, and in addition reveal the many levels of sacred soul service that animals demonstrate at any given time, including during disasters and pandemics, and even from the other side.

Part II, "The Sacred Partnership," is the heart of the book. You might want to prepare yourself for the expansion and inspiration these animals will surely leave on the doorstep of your heart. It is also likely that by the end of Part II you'll look at your animal companions with an even greater level of gratitude for how they have lovingly served you. The example stories in chapters 7, 8, and 9 highlight transformational soul journeys, including the way each animal is in service to their person, others, and what their gold nugget teaching is for you! These particular examples provide a deeper look into several remarkable partnerships and also contain journal prompts, rituals, and practices to guide your work alongside your animal companion.

Part III, "Your Sacred Work," will give you a myriad of ways—through the sharing of my favorite 5D practices—to achieve and hold a higher vibration so you can live an easier, 5D lifestyle alongside your animals. We all want to ease the journeys of our hardworking animal companions, and now you will have the tools to do so. In addition, I called upon industry experts to provide cutting-edge information on sound therapy and crystal therapy for both animals and people that I think you will love!

Perhaps you are unaware of your beloved animals' higher purpose in your life and are eager to learn more about those possibilities. Their deep, unwavering love for you will remain steadfast no matter where you are on your ascension path to 5D living. Each step of the way, and with utmost certainty, they will remind you that you are lovable and that you matter.

The journey we are about to embark upon will likely touch each facet of your life with animals. Upon the completion of reading this book, I hope you will look at your animals with a newfound respect. I *also* hope that you fully comprehend that you and your animal companions are copilots on the same flight to a higher dimension. Whatever this book helps you to tap into for your growth, know that it is written from the heart and infused with an abundance of love from the animal kingdom.

May the teachings and incredible animals in this book bring you a new level of healing such that you feel empowered and safe enough to shine your light brighter and share your unique gifts with the world.

PART I

Their Sacred Purpose

When we truly understand that we are all part of one another, that we are all in this together, and when we truly live from our heart's wisdom, we can no longer tolerate creating conditions that could bring suffering for any soul.

JUDITH CORVIN-BLACKBURN

1

What Is an Animal Wayshower?

The creatures that inhabit this earth, be they human beings or animals, are here to contribute, each in its own particular way, to the beauty and prosperity of the world.

DALAI LAMA

The term *wayshower* is being used with more and more frequency as humanity continues its evolutionary journey toward embracing and embodying higher levels of consciousness. Wayshowers are lightworkers with a strong commitment to serve others and share their gifts with all those who might benefit. Many wayshowers are driven at a soul level to partake in the creation of a new Earth, one that is grounded in community, harmony, compassion, and love.

Wayshowers can also embody the namesake through unassumingly inspiring others by living an authentic, positive, loving lifestyle. As a result of a wayshower's ability to hold a higher vibration of light and more 5D love-based virtues, others are drawn to and inspired to "be like them." You might be thinking now of the people you feel guided to emulate and model yourself after due to a deep respect for how they live, how they treat others, and how they make you feel.

But what about your beloved animal companions? Perhaps the very beings you share your home and heart with are also worthy of your attention and respect for how they model living in a higher state of consciousness and are connected to the greater whole. Perhaps their soul mission is to exemplify compassionate and loving traits to raise your consciousness to the next level and be your ascension guides to the higher dimensions. Perhaps they are the best representations of how to be a wayshower that you will ever rub noses with.

As lightworkers and wayshowers, many times our beloved companions are intentionally choosing to serve humanity in ways that might not always be obvious. One of the earliest memories a recent class attendee recalled was of her childhood family cat, Max. Christine shared that as an infant, she had a heightened level of fear of being alone in her crib. Her parents unknowingly contributed to her fears through their "let her cry it out" philosophy, but their beloved cat Max always responded to her need to be nurtured. Each and every night, he'd leap into her crib and curl up next to her, creating the safety and comfort baby Christine desired.

The nighttime fears persisted into her childhood years, and as Christine headed toward her room at bedtime, Max would predictably run to meet her in the hallway as if to say, *I'm here! Everything is going to be okay!* and then he'd snuggle up with her until she felt safe and fell asleep.

So, let's look deeper into Max's selfless acts during Christine's childhood. Max, in his mission to serve Christine and alleviate her fears, is expressing one of the endless ways that animal wayshowers reveal themselves. Through his dependable nurturing, a part of her psyche learned that she was worthy of receiving love and comfort.

Christine revealed that her relationship with Max was pivotal in helping her to embody and emulate the qualities he so beautifully modeled. Even today, Christine is empathetic and compassionate to others' needs because she learned the importance of being heard and cared for by her childhood feline friend. Max changed the trajectory of how she responds to and relates to others! He was a crucial early influencer and role model in Christine's life through his high vibrational attributes. Can you imagine the countless times animals have positively enhanced children's emotional development?

✳ *Let us never underestimate the profound effects of the animals that we are blessed to share our lives with, and how they contribute to shaping who we are today and who we are becoming.*

Animal wayshowers are not only caretakers and healers, they can also dramatically shift our emotional development, teaching us that we are lovable and worthy of receiving love and are completely accepted—perceived flaws and all. There are countless people that never knew what it felt like to be loved unconditionally until they shared their life with an animal. I happen to be one of those people. Upon experiencing that intimate, vulnerable, beautiful feeling for the first time with a kitten named Khalua, a decades-old barricade of protection released from my heart—one that I wasn't aware was even there! This is at the heart of why people are magnetized to animals. It's truly extraordinary when you think about the enormity of their ability to help humans to experience love. Animals' contribution to the opening of humanity's hearts is unparalleled.

The reach of the animal wayshower depends on the sacred soul pilgrimage they designed *with* their person to engage in during this lifetime. The animal with an expanded reach of sacred service has an intention and higher purpose, at a soul level, to reach more beings that will benefit from their transformational gifts. And they have likely teamed up with a person who allows this to unfold. Many of these animals are indeed old souls.

All beings, regardless of where they are on their evolutionary journey, are sparks of the Divine and are here to utilize their unique and valuable gifts to cultivate the growth experiences their souls long for to assist in their ascension process. Many times, the animals that are expressing their wayshower virtues are utilized in healing circles, schools, nursing homes, or to assist those with medical needs like blindness or PTSD, to name a few.

✳ *Be it old or young souls, two or four legs, all beings have wayshower traits within them to activate and utilize on behalf of something greater.*

Sometimes animals are taking deeper dives into their own transformational journey alongside their person, for they are also on their evolutionary journey and reside at varying levels of ascension. One being that is holding a higher vibration and expressing more wayshower traits is not "better" than other beings that are at a different level of learning. Several examples of this "deeper dive" type of relationship are revealed in the second part of this book. And even more incredibly, your animal might be hosting the soul of one of your spirit guides or soul group peers that has agreed to serve you and others in a more expansive way. Almost always in these cases, the feeling of familiarity and the deep love bond between this pairing is off the chart.

In the pages ahead these aforementioned topics will be explored in more depth. You'll learn about 5D virtues and traits, the transformational pairing of animals and their people, and the many ways animals are guiding you to initiate a kinder, more peaceful way to navigate your life experiences.

You might be wondering about situations where animals are living in abusive or difficult situations. Many animal wayshowers have intentionally chosen to be in the center of challenging times and circumstances, for divine intention places them there to serve others through difficult periods or initiate feelings of empathy and compassion within their abuser. Each wayshower has their own way to illuminate the divine pathway for those they assist, such that they will be exponentially catapulted forward on their soul's evolutionary expedition.

Feeling Is Believing
Trudy's Story

I recall a heartwarming story shared from Cheryl Flanagan, the founder of Save the Horses rescue organization, about Trudy, a horse the organization rescued that had suffered unthinkable abuse. It was the worst case of abuse that Cheryl had ever seen. Trudy would tremble with paralyzing fear, terrified to be around people. Cheryl said that Trudy blew her breath so hard through her nostrils that it sounded like a freight train passing through a busy crossing.

Over time, Cheryl and the volunteers lovingly helped Trudy to warm up to people more, but her fears never went completely away. It was challenging to tend to her because she didn't want to be touched by people. Furthermore, her prior abuse had created vision problems that also contributed to her heightened level of fear. Ultimately one of her eyes had to be completely removed to lessen her pain, and she was technically blind in her other eye for the last seven years of life. Cheryl feared that Trudy would revert to exhibiting extreme levels of fear and anxiety when they made the decision to have her eye surgically removed. Instead, she appeared to lean into the help of her caregivers more and began to trust the knowing familiarity of their scents and energy.

For her own safety Trudy was in her stall much of the time, but she was frequently taken on guided walks by volunteers who loved her and were drawn to help this amazing soul that had been through so much. Through that deeply transformational time of having to depend on people even more, Trudy's presence seemed to console anyone caring for her and revealed her soul's higher purpose of being a wayshower for others. Cheryl shared that despite all that Trudy had endured, it seemed clear to her that Trudy had made a conscious choice to be the opposite of her abusers. Not once did she ever lash out to hurt anyone; even with being afraid, she was *always* kind.

Frequently, Trudy's caregivers and volunteers at the rescue center would offer to keep her company so she wouldn't feel lonely. What would always begin with the intention of helping Trudy quickly shifted as the volunteer would share that their time with her was transformative and healing for *them*. Just spending time with Trudy brought about a beautiful release of whatever

Trudy, Save the Horses founder Cheryl Flanagan,
and caretaker Roger Morton

was heavy on their hearts, and they'd leave feeling better . . .
lighter. Being with Trudy was likened to being in the presence of
grace. Years later, Cheryl still gets emotional talking about Trudy
and the hearts she opened and lives she changed, including
Cheryl's own. Trudy lived to be approximately thirty-three years
of age, and the last twenty-one of those she knew love, as did all
those fortunate to spend even a moment with her.

Trudy's life was not an easy one, but she was a brave and
powerful wayshower. She beautifully demonstrated for hundreds of people how to be in a place of grace and kindness,
regardless of past abuse. The methods and manner that each
animal wayshower has chosen to work are individual; no one
way is better than any other. Each soul's path is unique for how
it wants to be, grow, and evolve through its experiences—and

how it has designed each individual's life to unfold. Sometimes, like in Trudy's case, it can feel incomprehensible to understand why any being must suffer so another may become enlightened. The good news is that humanity is making progress in moving toward a 5D way of living, which means much less physical suffering. More on this topic in the next chapter!

Wayshowers and lightworkers have overcome many challenges during their evolutionary journey, which is exactly what allows them to show up as a teacher and guide in the manner they are in this life. It can be likened to a grandparent having wisdom that a young child hasn't yet acquired through their experiences. The presence of challenge or difficulty in any being's life is not necessarily a sign of personal purification needing to take place at a karmic level, but instead perhaps is a part of their mission to raise the vibration of others, like Trudy beautifully emulated. Many times, the animals that you feel a deep connection with have evolved through much adversity to reach the point where they can maintain a higher vibration and exhibit more wayshower qualities. Like a magnet, we are attracted to their immense capacity to give and receive love, acceptance, and compassion.

✳ *Once you feel the honesty of unconditional love,*
nothing else seems to measure up.

The Mayor of Kindness
Hilton's Story

Hilton was named for Hilton Head Island, the beloved vacation spot of his mom, Cindy. After taking time to grieve the loss of her previous dog companion, Cindy felt ready to adopt again. From the moment Cindy walked into the pet food store she noticed Hilton staring at her with a big smile on his face, and suddenly it was as if all of the other dogs disappeared into the background. She signed the adoption papers that very day.

From the first day he arrived in his new home, Hilton's calm, grounding presence made everything feel better. Hilton's old soul personality is one of complete acceptance and love for all beings. From day one, he exuded only kindness toward Cindy's three cats. Not long after she adopted Hilton, she went through a difficult period of her life and credits him for being the consistent grounding force that carried her through that time.

Cindy recalled an awful day several years ago when her neighbor's house caught on fire. Her neighbor, a mother of five children and many animals, flew into action. One by one, she

Hilton
receiving
love from a
neighbor

brought her two-legged and four-legged children to Cindy's house and dropped them off for safety. While Cindy was holding the neighbor's baby and speaking to the 911 operator, Hilton instinctively began ministering to the other children. His presence with the children consoled them, which softened their fears from the tragic event. After the neighbor's home was rebuilt, Hilton suddenly began appearing on their doorstep for visits—something he never did before. He'd formed an incredible relationship with the children and sought out the connection.

Hilton is affectionately known as the Mayor of High Point and often wears a bowtie to embody the title. Everyone stops to share some special time with him while he lies on his back in the front yard to get his belly rubbed. He insists on being outside so he can see "his people" every day, and they always feel better for having received Hilton's sweet love.

The same thing happens when Cindy and Hilton visit

Hilton headed to the beach

Hilton Head Island twice yearly. Hilton sits in his own beach chair and the locals and those that regularly visit the island run up and ask "Is that Hilton?" Cindy jokes that no one knows her name, but they all know Hilton. He is deeply loved by all that meet him because he is kind, accepting, and loves deeply in return.

✳　*Your animal is always showing you the way back to your heart.*

Animals fill us with so much light. They are not simply looking for a warm lap or a treat, they are our evolutionary partners and emissaries on our journey to 5D and beyond. These beautiful heroes and heroines skillfully exemplify transcendence on Earth. The path of a wayshower requires integrity and intentionality to maintain 5D habits and self-care, but you, and in turn your animals, will be rewarded with far more loving experiences and far less suffering.

✳　*Your animals always feel better when you feel better.*

Each and every person and animal have the courage within to embrace their "inner wayshower" for the greater good of all beings. Animals just make it look easy because a larger percentage of them have mastered the ability to maintain a higher frequency. The good news is that they are here to show you how to become proficient at utilizing your wayshower attributes too!

2

5D Consciousness Is in the House (or Barn)

Intuition is knowingness, and this field of unbounded knowing, of knowingness, is within each human being. You start tapping into that and it becomes an ocean of solutions.

DAVID LYNCH

Imagine walking into a room and, in the blink of an eye, you intuitively know each person's needs with laser accuracy. You sense who needs to be comforted, who needs to be nudged to get outside in nature to get grounded, and who needs help to release repressed emotions.

This is how most of our animal companions traverse through life each day . . . instinctively navigating in the fifth dimension of consciousness. Their innate sense to serve others is instinctively a part of their wiring. And they don't have to physically be in the same room with you to know what you need, what you are feeling, or to help you release your burdens. You could be on Mars and they would still know when you are feeling unlovable and want to help you shift into knowing the truth of how lovable you are. This intuitive way of being connected to others is common in fifth-dimensional living. Perhaps you might already be having similar 5D experiences!

A Wise Teacher
Cheri & Gamera

It was never on Cheri Hayashi's wish list to have a turtle companion, but it was definitely at the top of her young daughter's. When their family adopted Gamera, the red-eared slider aquatic turtle was merely the size of a dollar coin. Given that Cheri is an animal communicator and avid animal lover, it is apparent that Gamera incarnated to work *with* Cheri so they can serve others *together*. Cheri describes Gamera as a very wise soul. Those who are in tune with energy have shared that they unfailingly can sense Gamera's Divine presence. It feels as if she holds the key to ancestral knowledge and is sharing it through her vibration.

For the last thirteen years, Gamera has lived at the English school Cheri founded in Sapporo, Japan. As you might predict, the children are magnetized to Gamera, eager to connect with her. Over the years Cheri has repeatedly been awestruck as she observed Gamera work her old soul version of magic with the children. After gazing into Gamera's eyes with wonderment, the children are suddenly calmer and more peaceful. Cheri notices a tangible energy exchange between the child and Gamera, as if they are communicating at a soul level. An anxious child is suddenly more serene and grounded after connecting with this wise turtle.

Gamera has ministered to hundreds of children in her life. One might say that she is one of the teachers on staff at the school. She is living the life her soul intended so that she can

Gamera

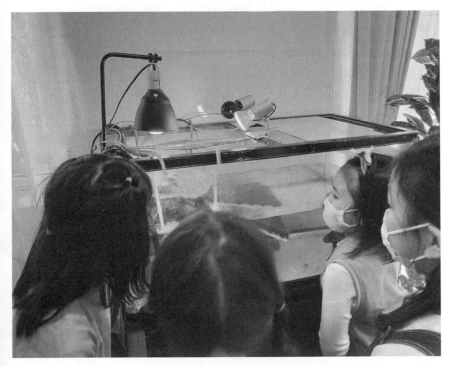

Students gazing at Gamera

serve Cheri's family and the students, who are all undoubtedly fortunate to receive her wisdom and gifts.

Animals are the ambassadors of 5D consciousness. Animals have always been our guides, assisting us as we travel the ascension path from 3D to 5D. These wise ascension guides have been showing us the way to embrace a way of living that transcends the duality of 3D into one that supports healing for other beings simply by holding a higher state of consciousness. This ability to alter others as a result of maintaining a higher frequency is what I call the *Transformational Healing Presence,* like Gamera beautifully demonstrates with the students.

We are all spiritual beings having a physical experience. Generally, animals merge their spiritual and physical realities together more graciously, which supports the retention of fifth-dimensional virtues. When all beings on Earth are habitually maintaining the attributes that arrive with 5D living, humanity, the animal kingdom, and our beautiful planet will be vibrating at a frequency not seen since the golden years of Atlantis. Fifth-dimensional virtues precipitate the natural unfolding of the path of the wayshower.

Let's dive into this coveted level of consciousness that animals have mastered, upheld, and sustained with ease and grace, for it holds significant benefits for you. It will also improve your communication with animals and enable you to receive their spiritual messages in ways that don't require them to have physical manifestations or negative behaviors to get your attention.

Fifth-dimensional consciousness is a way of *being* and living your life with more peace and harmony. All beings are ascending, be it consciously or unconsciously, through their quest to hold a higher vibration, or higher frequency. The vibration of your body, mind, and spirit determines the experiences you manifest and your reactions to them.

This is how Maureen St. Germain describes the fifth dimension in her book *Waking up in 5D.* "The fifth dimension is a vibrational frequency of unconditional love with the absence of fear, where compassion rules your emotions." Take a deep breath and read that sentence again! Yes! Let's pack light and move to 5D! The fifth dimension has been likened to experiencing heaven on Earth, and the good news is that it is available and attainable for *all* beings. Each and every person and animal is worthy of accessing and experiencing the higher dimensions.

This chapter will look deeper into the qualities and attributes that animals and humans can exhibit in 3D, 4D, and 5D to highlight their unique differences. In addition, I'll reveal which type of animal-human soul contract is likely to be operating within those dimensions. A soul contract is an agreement between two beings to expand their growth in this lifetime that has been created by the higher selves of both parties. All animal lovers are utilizing the growth that can be derived through partaking in animal-human soul contracts because of their ability to help you navigate the ascension process *with* your animals.

All beings can have 3D, 4D, *and* 5D experiences in any given day! The goal, however, is to live more consciously by habitually making 5D choices until it becomes your *new normal,* like most animal companions have already mastered. When you are perpetually maintaining a frequency of 5D consciousness, your animal companion will reap the benefits of your vibration, and you will *both* have more heart-opening, loving experiences. One of my favorite daily mantras is *God, help me to make 5D choices today!* Just stating this to the Universe will set in motion your intention to call in an easier way of being and living.

It might be helpful to understand the fifth dimension if we first take a walk through the third and fourth dimensions to reveal how each one differs and shows up for you and your animals.

While attending a spiritual retreat in 2004, I was feeling so connected that love was oozing out of my pores! Upon waking on the final morning, I sat up on the side of the bed and immediately noticed a huge spider on the ground about two feet away. It was a four-inch wolf spider or, as I call them, "east coast tarantulas." My first reaction was noticing how beautiful it was, and I even told her as much. We had a spiritual moment wherein we connected and I could feel her wonderful energy. She showed no sign of fear whatsoever. In fact, she seemed to be enjoying the encounter very much.

Then I began thinking about getting ready for my day alongside my new friend, and fear crept in. I glanced at my open suitcase next to her, and while I had no intention to bring about her demise, I also didn't want her crawling out of my suitcase when I got home. In just a few seconds time, my fears instantaneously escalated and my heart began racing. Then out of nowhere the spider suddenly jumped in fear, as if it was suddenly startled, and began running away as quickly as possible. It was as if she had received a life-or-death alert on her inner Siri.

My experience is a perfect example of how quickly your vibration and level of consciousness can shift between 5D and 3D. I will always remember how the spider intuitively sensed and reacted to the change in my energetic vibration.

The encounter still motivates me to watch my thoughts and unfounded fears so I can remember the importance of maintaining a 5D frequency. Everyone around us can feel our vibration, whether or not they are consciously aware of it.

✳ *The journey to another dimension is but a thought away.*

THE DUALITY OF 3D LIVING

It is well known that three-dimensional living can be . . . well, let's say, challenging. In this dimension you identify with the polarity birthed from fear and control, which gives way to victimhood, lack, attachment, and suffering. It is helpful to remember, though, that your Higher Self and your animal's Higher Self intentionally incarnated and chose to experience the contrast available in this dimension for your personal growth. However, this absolutely does not mean that you must continue to hang out and set up camp in the third dimension!

It's highly likely that you (your soul) signed up during this momentous time in history to help our planet evolve to 5D consciousness. It can be difficult to conceptualize this though, due to so many beings, both two-legged and four-legged, that have experienced trauma, abuse, physical and emotional pain, and suffering in the third dimension. Lightworkers frequently incarnate to experience much contrast and quickly awaken to the truth of who they are and their soul's mission to help others heal and evolve.

While in the third dimension, we can discover the truth that we are all connected, which usually arrives by learning through contrast, or opposites. If you weren't shown empathy while in an abusive relationship, hopefully you garnered the value of giving and receiving empathy because of the unfortunate experience, instead of emulating the abuser, which actually happens with more frequency. This process is a very effective way to learn how to embrace these higher vibrating emotions, and we all knew this coming into this earthly experience. Alas, it is in the third dimension that we can awaken and remember who we are and begin to develop the healthy internal parenting skills needed for the fourth dimension.

Codependency thrives in 3D. Whether you are in a codependent relationship with an animal or person, know that it is rooted in an unresolved wound of abandonment within you both. It takes concerted effort to heal your abandonment wound to allow in healthier relationships that don't require either the need to be needed or the need to be dependent on the love and support of animals or people to feel good. Know that animals are happy to oblige your timing and wherever you are on your transformational healing journey. This particular wound, left unhealed, is the one that makes it especially difficult to release the animal when it is their time.

Aggressive reactions, or "triggers," which are typically rooted in an unhealed betrayal wound, are also rampant in 3D for animals and people who haven't begun accessing the higher dimensions of spiritual support. All perceived "bad" people or animals are simply the soul agitators you called in for your own growth. The reactors are in turn creating invasiveness wounds in countless others. Emotional wounds, and their protective patterns, are created and established in 3D, along with the distorted self-preservation beliefs the psyche creates. All five emotional wound profiles, and how to identify and heal them, are detailed in my first book, *Soul Healing with Our Animal Companions.*

The physical soul contracts, or Physical Agreements,* between people and animals are rooted in 3D. These are the contracts wherein animals absorb and mirror your physical manifestations in hopes of helping you feel better and raise your awareness around energy transference. Raising your awareness of this instinctively guides you to 4D, where the deep innerwork can commence. In my twenties and thirties my animals frequently had the exact same physical ailments that I contracted, and I was clueless as to how to heal my underlying emotional wounds. At the time I knew it had to be more than a coincidence, but I had to wait until I awakened to higher frequencies of possibilities at the age of forty before I realized the depth of what my beloved companions did on my behalf.

Many times, Projection Agreements are playing out in this dimension. Projection Agreements can awaken you to how you might unknowingly be projecting unresolved wounds and distorted beliefs onto your animal. Old patterns can rise to the surface when your animal has a behavior that triggers an old wound. For instance, perhaps you did not feel heard by one or both of your parents. If your animal doesn't appear to be listening to you, they might inadvertently receive some of your repressed emotions that weren't expressed to your parents.

Many animal abusers, unfortunately, are projecting their pain and unresolved issues onto their animals. All animal abuse is derived in the third dimension. Sadly, there are many

---

*To read more about the soul agreements, also known as *soul contracts,* between humans and animals, see my book *Animal Soul Contracts.*

apathetic people stuck in the third dimension that do not yet respect animals or know they are sentient beings. Animals have taken the brunt of humanity's expression of their unresolved wounds for far too long. This is changing, though, as more and more people are waking up, doing their inner work, and taking a stand to protect animals like never before. As I write this, there have been huge leaps forward with new laws passed to charge animal abusers and a huge push for all shelters to be no-kill. In March 2021, Los Angeles became the largest no-kill shelter city in the United States. These positive changes contribute to raising the planet's vibration. Focusing on the growth and positive movement forward helps you to retain a higher vibration.

THE 4D BRIDGE

The fourth dimension is the unavoidable vehicle that moves us out of the duality and suffering that inhabits 3D to the land of ease and grace in 5D. Think of it as a bridge that beckons the spiritually awakened to heal and relinquish possibly lifetimes of pain and trauma, while simultaneously providing the joy and blissful feelings of 5D. If we can think of it that way, wow, what an amazing opportunity we have in this lifetime to be awake and do the heavy lifting our soul desires to ease our future experiences!

Much of the time we land squarely in 4D through a spiritual awakening or event that brought us to our knees and shifted our beliefs. For me it was an awakening through my mother's final six weeks of life, wherein she would share conversations she had with loved ones on the other

side, along with the passing of all three of my animal companions within several months' time. That's the year that I
was launched like a rocket into the transformational fourth
dimension due to my repressed childhood abuse and trauma
memories suddenly rising to the surface and into my awareness. While it was a gut-wrenchingly unforgettable year, I
will forever be grateful for it because it led me to my soul's
purpose. One thing is for certain, whatever it was that
shifted your path to look at things differently and begin
your ascension into the fourth dimension, your soul orches-
trated it all for your highest and best.

Animals are right beside you every step of the way while
you go through this beautiful purification process. They also
want to lighten their load from prior 3D wounding, and
oftentimes people must take the reins of their own healing
journey before animals can begin releasing their own wounds.

There can still be polarity and emotional wounding in
4D but it's intentional, and it either drives you into the lower
dimensions to heal something specific or lifts you up to 5D to
clear it without suffering. In the last few years, humanity as a
whole is stirring up old collective wounds to reveal and heal
them. Everything seems to be rising from the shadows into
the light. The emotional healing that transpires in the fourth
dimension is necessary for the collective's ascension process.

The fourth dimension is where the animal-human
Emotional Wound Agreements work their transformational
magic, which paves the way to physical and emotional wellness. Accessing the courage to begin an inner healing journey
is what propels us into 4D. Then the integration process energetically allows us to step out of victim consciousness and into

the loving neutrality of the fifth-dimensional frequency.

Karma can be cleared and accumulated on multiple dimensions. However, in the fourth dimension I see more negative karma completed and cleared—and along with this clearing, I've observed a passionate desire to create *positive* karma.

Compassion for the self and others is particularly beneficial for the transformation that unfolds in this sometimes frenetic dimension. In essence, we utilize the transitional fourth dimension to assist in our journey to 5D, and while there we might feel "all shook up." While in 4D we are able to touch, taste, and feel the higher vibrational emotions, which further motivates us upward and onward to 5D. To summarize, we utilize the fourth dimensional polarity to *shake loose* our attachments, patterns, and addictions that no longer serve us. This is the cleansing and purification dimension that moves us from victimhood to empowerment. Without it, we are indeed stuck in the mud of duality and lack.

THE EASE AND GRACE OF 5D LIVING

> *You are not a drop in the ocean. You are the entire ocean in a drop.*
>
> RUMI

There is a stream of consciousness connecting and unifying every living being, including animals and nature, and we feel this in every fiber of our being in the fifth dimension. As our beautiful planet continues shifting and holding higher vibrations, we are all exposed to 5D and even 6D frequencies with increasing regularity, which dramatically enhances our sense of safety and peace. While experiencing 5D frequencies, we feel and know in our hearts that we are not alone, and this knowing, in and of itself, is a treasured spiritual gift that soothes the soul.

Living in fifth-dimensional consciousness with regularity means everything is easier. It is almost fearless in 5D because you can more accurately intuit situations, and there is no suffering. You feel more joy, love, compassion, connection, and confidence and are able to see the blessings and gifts in everything and have unlimited creativity. We've all felt the vibration of 5D consciousness each time we feel gratitude, the kind that opens your heart and your eyes well up and you suddenly realize that everything is a miracle. Every time you feel unconditional love, deeply connect with your animal, hold a newborn baby, connect with the purity and essence of nature, or feel utter and complete joy through laughter, you are experiencing the grace that *is* 5D living.

While in this wonderful dimension alongside your animals, you will likely have many Symbolism Agreements operating with your companions, wherein they are enacting and reacting to your needs instantaneously, as are the animals in nature. If you need to meditate to get connected, they might lead you to your meditation chair or go sit there themselves and beckon you to join them! There are so many beautiful synchronistic ways animals can provide assistance with your frequency when you are awake to see the higher purpose in their actions.

The Pinnacle Teaching Agreements are also held in the fifth dimension. These are the highest vibrational teachings possible from your animals. Usually, they are modeling or mirroring the pinnacle virtues for you to realize that these golden attributes are also a part of you. Some of the pinnacle teaching virtues animals are emulating for us are compassion, acceptance, authenticity, truth, forgiveness, empathy, faith, trust, grace, gratitude, vulnerability, and, of course, unconditional love.

These are holy, sacred emotions filled with light and love, and our animal companions selflessly reflect and hold them for us until we awaken to the realization that we hold these virtues within ourselves as well. It is amazing, when you think about it, how these beautiful creatures come into our lives to rescue *us* and show us the way to 5D living. They are possibly the only beings that you've ever given access to your heart and trusted enough for them to show you what it feels like to be loved unconditionally.

While living in this level of consciousness there is a tangible feeling of connection to all beings. This is when *you* become the one who walks into a room of people and can intuitively read each person's needs and emotions with accuracy. It is common in 5D to have heightened levels of psychic gifts like telepathy, clairvoyance (spiritual sight into other dimensions), and clairsentience (feeling and sensing others energy and emotions), to name a few.

As you know if you've had more than one animal companion in your life, each animal's higher sense skill sets vary, much like humans. Every animal exhibits psychic gifts due to their 5D attributes. Each species is a bit different but having psychic gifts is common for those with 5D consciousness.

TRANSFORMATIONAL HEALING PRESENCE

Earlier in this chapter you learned about Gamera the turtle who has the ability to calm and soothe children by holding 5D attributes and utilizing them for the greater good. We often overlook the profound gift of humbly emanating *Transformational Healing Presence*. I've known many animal lovers who have shared that their animals embody this beautiful fifth-dimensional ability. In each and every case, the people described the animal as being more detached, but the person also undeniably senses the animal's strength and ability to transcend the emotions in a room by unpretentiously being fully present and holding a 5D frequency. Even more, there is loving *purpose* to their sacred work. Their loving presence is understated elegance and grace rolled into a bliss-filled union of the heart.

There is no need for codependent relationships in the fifth dimension because you (and your animals) know that all of your needs will be taken care of and you are simply grateful for the journey. So, when one of your animals appears to be a little more detached, and you sense a grounded greatness radiating from them, know that they are living in a higher vibration, and they are serving you, and others, through their Transformational Healing Presence. It reminds me of when Buddhists speak of the art of nonattachment. Nonattachment is a 5D spiritual superpower to be beholden. Most gurus and spiritual teachers have mastered this 5D trait, along with most cats!

Many animals have incarnated to hold this loving presence as part of their sacred service to humanity. Always express gratitude to these incredible creatures that have gone through much to achieve this state of being. Their souls don't want a toy or a treat as a way to thank them, for material recognition is not the way of those who embody 5D consciousness. The highest form of flattery for these incredible wayshowers is for you to emulate their ways.

- Tend to your own vibration and strive to maintain a 5D frequency.
- Listen without judgement.
- Accept everyone as they are and wherever they are on their journey as right and perfect for them.
- Love others unconditionally without trying to control or fix them.
- Live authentically. Be true to yourself by intentionally connecting to your Divine nature.
- Hold a safe, loving space for the highest and best of all.
- Allow your vibration to organically serve others.

And for anyone thinking that they haven't yet discovered their spiritual gifts, or how to serve the collective in a grander way . . . know that you may already be doing what your soul arrived to do through your Transformational Healing Presence. This ability, in and of itself, is creating a powerful, high vibrational wake around you in the collective consciousness, and I thank you. If we all strive to create a 5D loving presence within, we lighten the load for all beings.

The Magical Guru
Hope & Magic

There's no mistaking the fact that Magic knew what he wanted. Hope drove to the farm looking to adopt a spotted horse, but from the moment she walked into the pasture, Magic made his presence known. He confidently followed her around as if saying, *There's no need to get to know any of these other horses. I'm the one you came to meet.* Magic was persistent in his quest to get Hope to recall that their meeting was pre-destined, and they had spiritual work to do together. Hope immediately sensed a warm familiarity about his energy on that very first day when their souls recognized each other.

Upon arriving at his new home, the bond between them was undeniable. It was as if their hearts had known and loved each other for a very long time. If Hope is sad, Magic instinctively gets still and holds space for her to lean into his healing presence. From the very first day, and without any hesitancy, Hope's other horses allowed Magic to lead and protect them. He leads them not with aggression or assertiveness, but by the simple cock of an ear that relays to the other horse what he wants, and they intuitively know they can trust him and that he's got their back.

Magic is very grounded and brave, and one can sense his inner strength and sovereignty. He doesn't need or require affection to feel fulfilled because he resides in the fifth dimension. Much like an enlightened guru, his mere presence commands attention and respect. Similarly, as other horses that have mastered the ability to maintain a higher vibration, his energy field is very expansive and can extend to the size of Hope's entire farm.

Hope has hosted many Mayan Fire Ceremonies and sweat lodges on her sacred land. Sometimes during these events Magic appears out of nowhere running like the wind and circles the cer-emonial gathering of people. Several intuitive clairvoyants that attended one or more of the ceremonies have independently stated that they saw a Native American chief riding Magic during

Magic

his sacred run. Attendees sensed that Magic was intentionally creating a protective boundary around the ceremonial gathering to allow a sacred purification to unfold.

During women's group circles that were facilitated on Hope's property, Magic would respectfully and honorably greet each woman. It was obvious how his energy changed to adapt to the individual needs of each one, such that he could appropriately respond and minister to them. Magic communicates to the soul of each person in a way that 5D consciousness allows. He is a master healer and wayshower through holding a Transformational Healing Presence. His name perfectly suits him, as he is indeed magical in every way possible.

Tools for Creating 5D Relationships with Your Animal Companions

1. When your animals follow your guidance, instead of saying *Good boy* or *Good girl,* say *Thank you.* Ask them kindly to do something versus nudging them physically. The 5D "reward" for positive behavior is expressing gratitude and unconditional love.

2. Remove the word "bad" from your vocabulary with them. This word has negative 3D energy attached to it and isn't helpful in turning their behavior around. As much as possible, given that each situation demands a potentially different solution, diffuse the situation, and don't give attention or energy to the undesired behavior. Instead, redirect them and focus on any small, positive change in the right direction with gratitude and love.

3. Practice telepathy with them. Your animals are already reading your thoughts and feelings (also known as

your energy) so practicing with more intention to intimately connect with them energetically can dramatically enhance your relationship. Show them visuals (intentional thought with feelings) of the desired behavior you seek versus what you don't want them to do. This is a powerful way to communicate with your animals and is common in 5D consciousness. You might also want to take an animal communication course to enhance this skill set.

4. Seek the higher purpose in their actions. Take a step back and consciously shift to 5D (observer mode) to interpret their actions, behaviors, and issues as a message for you. They are always mirroring and reflecting some aspect of you, and they are endlessly wanting to serve your ascension process.

5. Resist projecting your emotions onto them. When you have pent-up emotions, move them out in healthy ways. If you find yourself being short with them, that's your cue that you've got some emotions that are coming up! Moving out the anger, frustration, or agitation in healthy ways will preserve and maintain the 5D integrity of your relationship, and then they don't have to absorb your unresolved emotions.

6. Use only positive labels and names for your animals. Three-dimensional programming is quick to give others negative labels via name-calling and stereotyping certain behaviors or appearances, which contributes to more 3D experiences for you both. Animals will embody the energy of the names and labels you give them, so choose wisely.

7. Invite your animals into your meditation or sacred prayer time. You can do this verbally or telepathically. It matters not if the animal is with you physically, in another room, or in the barn. They can still join you to receive the positive energy available while meditating, and this is a great tool to help you both achieve the transformational results you came together to bring about.

Take a deep breath and imagine that it is indeed possible for people and animals to ascend and experience the freedom of an authentic 5D lifestyle. Feel it in every fiber of your being. Take another breath with intention to sense and feel the 5D frequency even more intimately.

The time is now to embrace 5D living through the authentic essence that *is you.* Your incredible animals are here to assist you in the journey from 3D to 5D consciousness. Acknowledging the role animals are playing in our evolution will contribute to raising the collective consciousness. Enacting what they have modeled for us is the best way to honor their sacrifices on our behalf.

I close this chapter with a question. In this time of great potentiality to hold higher frequencies than ever before, our animal companions want to show us the way to our hearts and lift us into a 5D reality, *if* we are ready to raise our awareness and level of consciousness. Are you ready?

3

The Light Warriors of the Animal Kingdom

We all have a spiritual purpose, a mission,
that we have been pursuing without being fully
aware of it, and once we bring it fully into
consciousness, our lives can take off.

JAMES REDFIELD

It's beyond miraculous when you stop to consider how each person is drawn to perform a particular trade, role, or form of service. From truck drivers to musicians to scientists to healers and wayshowers, humanity's needs as a whole are met through each and every person's contribution to the collective. Each person's role is an important cog in the wheel of our lives, as there is a higher purposeful plan to ensure that the planet and its inhabitants have the best environment possible to support their physical and spiritual needs. As influenced as we all can be by those around us, our gifts, skill sets, and who we are at our core are uniquely and divinely different. You are an original! And you matter.

It is fascinating to look at the animal kingdom from a higher perspective, too, and the different roles animals play in the greater good of all on Earth. Each species has its own distinctive traits, strengths, gifts, and function of great significance in the circle of life. And still, every creature is unique and beautiful and divinely different. And each one matters. Each being also has a *spiritual* purpose that only it can fulfill.

Animals that have chosen, at a soul level, to live alongside us truly are the *light warriors* on the front lines of the animal kingdom's mission and contribution to raise the vibration of the collective consciousness. Aiding in humanity's ascension process is indeed a courageous undertaking! Anyone in animal rescue work is very aware of how brave and bold this choice is, given the amount of people yet to raise their level of awareness enough to have compassion and respect for all animals. There is an unfortunate reality that many animals are abused and even come to their demise due to their service and self-sacrifice to the very people they are trying to help. It is important to remember that there is always a Divine plan and the kind and committed people who lend a hand and rally around these animals are beautifully fulfilling *their* higher purpose and helping to balance the karma between us.

My admiration for domesticated animals frequently brings me to tears. I hold a deep reverence for their bravery in carrying out their part in helping us to heal and evolve. Where would we be without the horses, camels, and oxen that literally moved civilization from a nomadic to a migratory species? Animals have bravely been driving humanity's evolution for millions of years, and they deserve our heartfelt respect and gratitude. They connect us. They free us. They heal us. And they show us how to love ourselves and others.

✳ *Animals are beacons of universal light that have chosen to become domesticated for a reason. And that reason is us.*

These incredible luminaries are deeply committed to their soul mission to raise awareness and contribute to our ascension. Many of these light warriors are true masters in the methods they utilize to awaken their people to delve into their emotional wounds and heal them at the core. They will fight for you in ways no one else has.

Among other things, they courageously hold and mirror their humans' emotional wounds and traumas until their humans awaken and begin an inner healing journey, which promotes more fifth-dimensional experiences. With the physical and emotional risks associated with 3D living, our animal companions still radically agreed to stand in the light, *and* in the dark, on behalf of our shared evolution. This is an extremely high level of service!

In my twenties and thirties, I was frequently ill due to having a plethora of repressed childhood traumas and emotional wounds, and my three beloved cat companions habitually had physical issues too. I clocked in more than my share of time visiting doctors and veterinarians during that period of my life. Having a multitude of physical ailments felt normal since my mother modeled this common 3D choice to focus on the physical. Given that they were my first experience with unconditional love, there wasn't anything I wouldn't do for them to improve their health. Back then, I was dependent on my animals to feel loved.

As I reflect now, it's easy to see how my cats were advocating for me to look at "my stuff" through their mirroring and absorption of my issues. They were lightworkers that agreed to create a revolution in my soul and show me the way to a new level of consciousness. When Khalua, Bailey, and Vasi were eleven, eight, and six years of age, I had a spiritual awakening and, within a few months' time, all three of them transitioned back to the other side. Having fulfilled their sacred purpose, they got the wings they certainly earned, and I imagine more than a few heavenly high fives for their profoundly positive impact on my life. These three beautiful light beams changed the trajectory of my life so I could live authentically and feel more love than I knew was possible. Surely there is a heavenly hall of fame for animals that have mastered the ability to help those that are not yet capable of allowing in healing, love, and guidance from themselves or others.

It's been many years since then but occasionally I still have the need to recite the Ho'oponopono prayer to forgive myself for what they absorbed and endured on my behalf, even if I believe that they willingly signed up for the gig. The thought of being the cause of any suffering for our companions is a difficult notion for us animal lovers to shoulder. I will forever be grateful to them for their noble commitment to my growth.

Ho'oponopono is a beautiful Hawaiian Huna practice of resolution and forgiveness. The exercise of reciting the Ho'oponopono prayer is a wonderful tool to release any regret that has been heavy on your heart and that seeks reconciliation. According to Ulrich Dupree, author of *Ho'oponopono*, the origin of Ho'oponopono might just reach as far back as Atlantis, Lemuria, and the High Vedic Culture. When recited together, the four Ho'oponopono statements hold a high frequency of light, healing, and empowerment. I believe that all forgiveness is self-forgiveness.

Suggestion: Close your eyes, put your hands on your heart, and repeat the prayer until you feel a shift of energy.

I'm sorry.

Please forgive me.

Thank you.

I love you.

Your animals are relentless in their duties to usher in 5D consciousness to relieve your emotional pain. They are fierce and determined warriors when it comes to helping you to remember why your soul enlisted them for the deep transformational shadow work you crave in this life. If you are one of the millions that get emotionally close to your animal companions, know that you teamed up with them for your shared personal growth, and your pairing is predestined. There can be substantial physiological or emotional shifts through your conscious work together.

The Advocate
Barb & Gidget

Intervertebral disc disease (IVDD) is fairly common in dachshunds, and there are varying levels of the disease that range from the dog having impaired mobility to complete paralysis. Barbara Techel was all too familiar with caring for dogs with IVDD because she'd previously shared her heart and home with two adopted dachshunds. Barbara and her canine companions loved educating others about the disease and helping people to understand that dogs with this disease can have a great quality of life for many years. She knows firsthand that these sweet and lovable dogs are so worth the extra care they require.

After Barbara's second adopted dachshund, Joie, transitioned, she knew beyond a shadow of a doubt that she wanted to adopt another IVDD dog that would benefit from her knowledge and experience about the disease. On a whim she decided to jump on petfinder.com to scroll through the available dogs. As soon as Gidget's adorable photo popped up, Barbara instantly knew she was the one! Three months later, seven-year-old Gidget flew from Nevada to Wisconsin to begin a new chapter with her kind and loving mom.

From the very beginning, Barbara felt a deep kinship with Gidget, as if they'd known each other for a long time. Barbara always got the impression that there was an ocean of wisdom behind Gidget's deep soulful eyes. Over the years, Gidget habitually wanted to sit on Barbara's lap. While there, she would often tilt her head to the side and intently stare into her mom's eyes, as if looking into the depths of her soul and trying to communicate *something* of utmost importance. Barbara said it felt somewhat invasive and at times made her feel uncomfortable . . . as if she had an unconscious desire to *not* discover what it was Gidget was trying to relay.

In addition to her impaired mobility, Gidget developed seizures after moving in with Barbara and her husband. Barbara was very aware that this was a spiritual message for *her* since it was a new issue. Our animals frequently use behaviors or physical manifestations as a way to give us important messages. Barbara sensed that Gidget was helping her to "shake something loose" but had no idea what it was.

Gidget also had chronic urinary tract infections, and after

many years of 24/7 care, her constant physical needs were wearing on Barbara. One day everything came to a head and Barbara was feeling overcome by it all. She was beyond overwhelmed and exhausted, and she decided to reach out to a friend for advice. The friend lovingly defended and advocated for Gidget's life, certain that what was happening between the two of them was part of a Divine plan.

That was just what Barbara needed to hear to prompt her repressed emotions to erupt from the center of her being. Her wounded child was enraged because she longed for someone to advocate for *her*. An abundance of anger, pain, and sorrow that had longed to be free for decades all came flowing out. It seemed that Barbara was *shaking something loose!*

Since the age of twenty-nine, Barbara repeatedly had a vision that would flash in her mind that spontaneously made her feel nauseous and uneasy. She would always quickly dismiss it, not wanting to look at it. In the midst of her intense emotional release, she suddenly realized that the vision was a childhood memory of being inappropriately touched when she was a child by someone she should have been able to trust. This realization prompted a deep inner healing journey for Barbara to heal and love this young part of herself.

All of a sudden it was crystal clear that Gidget had always been *her* advocate! At a soul level, Gidget had repeatedly triggered Barbara's invasiveness wound and the distorted belief that the only choice was to suffer and endure what she was going through, which mirrored her abused inner child's feelings. She loved Barbara so much that her Higher Self agreed to help her to activate and expose her childhood wound. During the next and final year of Gidget's life, they grew closer than

Barb and Gidget.
Photo by Lisa A. Lehmann.

ever before. The anxiousness that was often in the center of their relationship had transformed into a deep inner peace.

Barbara's new level of awareness regarding the magnitude of Gidget's teachings fill her with love and endless gratitude to this day. Gidget is a courageous master healer and wayshower. Barbara went on to write a memoir about Gidget's impact on her life.

Gidget and Barbara's love story conveys the depth our animals willingly go to on our behalf. Your animals are helping you because of their deep and profound love for you. They see and love every single aspect of you. And I know that goes both ways. Take a moment to reflect on the manner in which your animal companion might be directing your attention to look at something deeper within yourself. Is there a behavior they have that makes you feel uncomfortable? Are they triggering a particular reaction and emotion as a result of one of their behaviors or habits?

If so, try meditating on what might be behind your reaction. Keep peeling back the layers of your thoughts until you get to the core of the issue, as if you are observing yourself from a higher perspective. You might need to do this exercise several times before you discover what your animal has been helping you to tap into for your highest and best. Ask for spiritual help in getting to the root of your animal's message, and then watch your dreams, feelings, and thoughts during meditation.

Not on My Watch
Anielle & Pepper

Pepper and her mom, Anielle Reid, have had a deep and loving soul bond since the moment they laid eyes on each other. Anielle describes Pepper as her *familiar*. Pepper is a chill, self-assured, and happy dog who beautifully emulates many 5D virtues. She loves deeply. She is always kind. And she unfailingly stands in her authentic truth to do what feels right for her, which Anielle realizes is one of her key teachings.

Early last year Anielle came to the agonizing decision to begin divorce proceedings, move out of her home, and find a place of her own. But interestingly, whenever she was about to leave the house to go look at apartments, Pepper would suddenly begin limping and literally stop walking. With utmost concern, Anielle rushed Pepper to the veterinarian's office, who gave feedback that her physical issue can sometimes happen with her breed. Each time her beloved companion would abruptly be stricken with the inability to walk, Anielle would become tormented with concern and worry—and be too afraid to leave her. Ultimately, she would change her plans to tend to Pepper.

Quite curiously when Anielle's focus shifted from looking for an apartment, Pepper "miraculously" recovered and began walking normally and even running again! It was only when Anielle was serious about finding a new place that Pepper would out of the blue begin limping and refuse to walk, which would without fail send Anielle into a heightened state of worry and fear, and then she'd change her plans.

On two different occasions Anielle found an apartment and paid a deposit, only for it to fall through in some way. And throughout the process Pepper's physical symptoms continuously haunted her with concern. Finally, Anielle took a step back and observed what had been occurring from a higher perspective. That's when she connected the dots regarding Pepper's "sudden" loss of movement and could undeniably see that she'd been intentionally intervening to steer her in another direction.

Anielle reevaluated her decision to move out, thanks to

Anielle and
Pepper

Pepper, and she and her husband worked through their issues. Their relationship has grown stronger and more loving. Since they made the decision to strengthen their marriage and stay together, Pepper has been happier than ever before, and she hasn't limped once since that time. Pepper intentionally embarked on a purposeful mission to bring healing and love into the heart of Anielle's marriage, in her own ingenious way.

Anielle and her husband agree that it was their amazing light warrior dog Pepper who fought for their marriage and created exactly the type of distraction Anielle needed to shift her thoughts and her course of action.

Pepper's clarity, commitment, and connection are extraordinary. She unabashedly guided Anielle and her husband to do the necessary work that would bring about a much-needed vibrational shift in their relationship. Pepper beautifully demonstrates how we are in partnership with our companions and how incredibly important their roles are in our ascension process. Animal wayshowers and lightworkers are always in sync with our energy and will do everything they can to encourage the growth our souls aspire to achieve.

Perhaps you've had an animal companion that went out of its way to divert your attention too. Take a few moments to reflect on a current or past situation with your animals. Seek the higher perspective and motivations of their purposeful actions and perhaps you'll have an aha moment!

Time to Work
Marilyn & Sophie

Marilyn shared with friends she'd met for lunch that she had opened up a yellow pages telephone book that morning and it flew open to a page that had an ad about a new animal rescue center nearby. It had been nearly eighteen months since Marilyn and her husband Terry had lost their previous dog, and while there wasn't an urgent need to get another canine companion, Marilyn is not one to look the other way when there are serendipitous signs from the universe. Her friends agreed and off they went to the new no-kill rescue center to meet the adoptable dogs! Once she saw Sophie, who'd only arrived at the facility an hour earlier, it was love at first sight. Sophie's playful six-month-old energy was so magical and fun, which mirrored Marilyn to perfection.

Sophie seamlessly adjusted to her new surroundings with such ease that it felt as if she'd always lived there and been a part of their family. She eagerly joined Marilyn during her daily meditation practice, in addition to participating in the angel circles Marilyn facilitated. Sophie always exhibited and aligned with 5D attributes. She was independent, grounded, and confident in who she was, and while not warm and fuzzy, she loved to play by herself and be outside in nature.

When Sophie was about a year old, Marilyn's ninety-year-old mother-in-law, Ruby, moved in with them, and that's when things changed. As if someone had turned on a light switch, Sophie's higher mission and purpose instantaneously revealed itself. While Ruby appreciated her son and his wife opening up their home to her, losing her independence was difficult, especially during those first few months. However, the saving grace was that Ruby had always been an avid dog lover, and she eagerly welcomed the love and comfort Sophie's high vibration provided.

From the moment Ruby moved in, Sophie's personality became more serious and intentional. She was committed to making sure that Ruby felt loved and taken care of. Every night after Marilyn went to bed, like clockwork, Sophie slipped downstairs to Ruby's room to hold sacred space for her all night long. Sophie had always objected to being around any type of noise, but she seemed to make an exception for Ruby's noisy oxygen concentrator. Sophie slept in Ruby's room for seven straight years, until Ruby was moved into hospice care. When Ruby was close to transitioning, Marilyn and Terry took Sophie to visit her. Sophie ran and jumped up on the bed, excited to see her dear friend and say their final farewells. Three days later Ruby transitioned.

Sophie is an exemplary example of demonstrating how significant the animal light warriors and wayshowers are in our lives. Without any fret or fuss, Sophie fully embraced her higher purpose to bring light and comfort to Ruby's final chapter of life. Sophie remained a cherished companion for three additional years, and then she reunited with her dear friend Ruby, who undoubtedly greeted her return to spirit with much love and gratitude.

Sophie

Sophie wonderfully exhibits that there is a Divine plan and purpose for *all* beings, and if we can learn to trust this knowing as truth, our animals' messages and teachings will reveal themselves more easily. When you trust in your animals' purpose, you will automatically begin operating from a new level of consciousness. This earthly experience is nothing to fear, as the animal light warriors beautifully demonstrate. The endless love from your light team and Higher Self is always available for you to tap into, and it matches the level of love you have for your animal kin. Lean into this earthly experience with the knowing that everything will be okay, and the Universe will effortlessly provide the benevolent outcomes your soul seeks.

An Expression of Gratitude

Take a moment to sink into the vibration of gratitude. Think of something you are grateful for, and then notice how your heart expands and your list of what you are grateful for multiplies. Now, thank the animals that you sense are around you. Thank them for the light and the shadow teachings that have exponentially impacted your life and enhanced your well-being. Thank them for the love you feel in your heart today that you never would have known was possible without them.

Let's also send gratitude to all the two-legged light warriors on the front lines of helping animals to lovingly transform their past emotional wounds and traumas, find their way to a better life, and to feel unconditionally loved. They are also heroes and heroines and deserve our heartfelt appreciation for their gallant efforts on behalf of the animal kingdom.

4

Wired to Serve

Although you appear in earthly form, your essence is pure consciousness. You are the fearless guardian of Divine Light.

RUMI

Do you remember how you felt when you held your newborn child for the first time? Or perhaps your grandchild, kitten, or puppy? There is a heart-opening moment that occurs when you connect to the purity of their essence, their soul, and know without a doubt that you love them like you have loved no other. Many times during these sacred spiritual encounters we are moved to tears, and the experience forever changes us. It is as if the newborn's very being permeates our soul and blasts through the protection around our hearts so we remember what it feels like to utterly and completely love another being. In that place filled with pure positive energy, we don't have an agenda nor are we lobbying to get our needs met. We are simply immersed in the field of consciousness that *is* love.

One of the reasons we experience these magical moments when we hold newborns is because our soul is responding to their high vibration. It radiates with the pureness of spirit, and in that moment a part of us remembers when we were also vibrating in the fearlessness of a higher frequency, and we long to be in that glorious state of superconsciousness again. When the newborn and its primary caretaker bond through a spiritual heart-to-heart fusion, they intuitively feel and read each other's energy, emotions, and needs. This loving way to connect using our higher senses is a common 5D way of communicating.

Animals also arrive in their earthly forms vibrating with a high level of consciousness from the other side, which allows them to easily communicate energetically with their birth mothers and their siblings. The biggest difference between people and animals is that animals instinctively trust and allow the flow of energy from the Divine and their Higher Self to guide them in the direction of their higher purpose *throughout their lives* because they maintain a higher vibration and continue to utilize their higher senses.

Because of their feeling nature, their presence in our lives is paramount for our emotional development and advancement in the way of the peaceful warrior. Domesticated animals are vital contributors for raising the planet's frequency to 5D. Think of it as if they are holding space on behalf of those who are enmeshed in third-dimensional duality. It is part of their mission to guide humanity to follow their lead (pun intended) to a gentler way of being and living, and how wonderful that the 5D frequency they maintain can profoundly benefit Earth and its inhabitants. They are wired to serve us from the moment they arrive!

Two Unique Healers
Shalan & Annie, Jenna & Kirby

Every Wednesday and Saturday, canines Jenna and Kirby have the pleasure of going to work with their moms. Shalan Hill

and Annie Pauley are extraordinary healers and the propri-
etors of a wonderful yoga studio and healing center. They've
always viewed their beloved dog companions as family and
cocreators on the journey. With much gratitude, Shalan and
Annie consider Jenna and Kirby to be an integral part of their
healing practice and recognize that all four of their souls
intentionally teamed up to serve others together.

From the moment they adopted Jenna, Shalan and Annie
knew that she was an old soul who had mastered the ability to
hold Transformational Healing Presence for those who need it.
They describe her as being a grid holder who grounds not only
others but also the energy in their home, their studio, and the
Earth. Jenna exhibits the fifth-dimensional traits of being confident and discerning, and she doesn't engage in codependent
relationships. She is very loving and works with each visitor of the
studio by teaching them gentle ways. She only responds to a loving, gentle touch, which teaches them to have more compassion
and empathy toward themselves and others.

Kirby has an engaging personality that wants everyone
to be aware of just how lovable and appreciated they are!
She enthusiastically engages with everyone and intentionally
shares her heart to bring joy to each and every interaction. She
is always ready to play and helps everyone tap into their inner
child! There have been many occasions when young children
have arrived at the studio with a little apprehension, and Kirby
immediately says, *Oh, I've so got this!* And before you know it,
the child is much more receptive to receiving hands-on healing
and bodywork.

While Jenna holds sacred space for the inner healing to
reveal itself, Kirby's healing methods are more experiential.

The differences in their methods are indicative of how beings are wired to serve others in their own unique way. Various approaches are always needed because everyone responds differently. These two lightworkers are the perfect healing team, which also beautifully reflects their moms.

Upon arrival, visitors familiar with the studio glance around the corner, looking for the canine healers who will predictably greet them with abundant enthusiasm. Jenna and Kirby are always eager and happy to support people in releasing anything that was heavy on their heart. Whether it is a recent loss in their life or an upsetting day at work, the change in people's mood and vibration is immediate after team Jenna and Kirby have ministered to them.

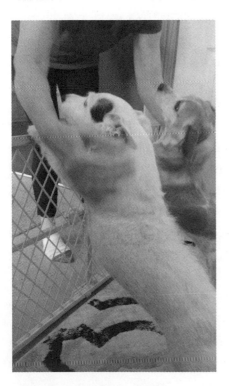

Jenna and Kirby at work

Annie and Jenna, Shalan and Kirby

Jenna and Kirby are beautiful depictions of wayshowers who entered their earthly bodies wired and ready to serve others. They are a blessing and a gift to all in their wake.

Your animal companions are prewired to serve you and the collective! They moved into your heart and home primed and ready to dive deeper into the spiritual teachings that will launch you both into the next dimension of consciousness.

Let's look at the broader picture of how your animal companions are wired and connected to each other and to you.

SPECIES FIELDS OF CONSCIOUSNESS

Every animal species is wired differently and incarnated with their own unique traits, gifts, and offerings to help raise the frequency of the planet and its inhabitants. There are many animal totem books and websites available to learn more about each animal species' innate, natural attributes and qualities. These resources give us generalized teachings to learn more about each species and tap into the spiritual and healing messages to integrate for our growth.

There is a stream of energy connecting all of the animals within each particular species. Held within the consciousness of this stream of energy is the species' higher purpose and intentions for its spiritual contributions to raising the frequency of our planet. Each and every animal's experiences, negative or positive, are collectively felt by all of their beloved relatives and peers. When an animal has more positive, loving experiences and is maintaining a 5D frequency, this benefits the entire species. In turn, that animal's overall contribution is more profound, and humanity is drawn to the light of that species. On the flip side, if animals are having repeated negative experiences, then they are all adversely impacted. This reduces the vibration in their stream of energy, which influences that species to react in undesirable ways.

Following are more details about the three most prevalent domesticated animals and their species' field of consciousness.

Dogs

All dogs are connected within the *Canine Consciousness* stream of energy that holds their collective purpose and intentions for serving humanity. As a whole, the intentions of the canines are to provide unconditional love, protection, loyalty, and support for children and for the *inner child* of adults. Within the Canine Consciousness energy field, there are subfields for the dogs bred with more specific intentions and purpose. Enhanced levels of protection, herding, and sporting are a few examples of subfield intentions.

A dog's capacity to provide unconditional love even while being abused is unparalleled. They willingly provide incredible support to their people who are undergoing an inner transformational journey from 3D to 5D. Like most domesticated animals you develop a close bond with, your dog will gladly absorb your repressed emotions and physical issues to ease your pain. These heaven-sent animals will remarkably hold space for you to develop higher levels of compassion and empathy for yourself and others. Dogs help us to connect to the wisdom of our hearts like no other being. If you allow a dog's unconditional love to awaken your heart, it will transform all of your relationships, beginning with the most important one . . . the relationship with yourself.

Those drawn to learn from dogs seek the 5D attributes
of unconditional love, safety, and sacred partnership.

Horses

Horses are highly evolved beings! Their energy fields can expand to an acre or more, which allows them to detect the slightest of incongruencies on the property and inform you if something needs your attention. The closer the bond with their guardians, the more engaged they are in their emotional inner healing journey. The *Equine Consciousness* stream of energy holds strong intentions to help people to feel empowered to move forward on their journeys to freedom, and these incredible beings are masters at holding Transformational Healing Presence for others. Yes, even from the barn or field, they are in tune with everything you are feeling and thinking and are tending to your well-being through your heart-to-heart connection. They have also been bred for specific purposes like riding, pulling, or plowing so there are many subfields of consciousness within the equine stream of energy.

Horses maintain a beautiful balance of heaven and Earth energy and are strong warriors of the light. These magnificent beings can show us how to nurture and maintain our connections to God and Gaia with utmost integrity.

Those drawn to learn from horses seek the 5D attributes of freedom, empowerment, and connection.

Cats

Cats are highly evolved enlightened beings that embody the honesty of 5D frequencies. The energy stream of *Feline Consciousness* holds intentions for cats to teach us about living independently. In addition, felines can adeptly balance their human's energy field, raise the vibration in your home, keep entities at bay, and teach those they share space with how to have loving detached acceptance of others. Cats are very connected to the spiritual realm, very psychic, and are also healers like other domesticated animals. All animals have varying degrees of psychic abilities, but there is a larger percentage of cats that express these qualities. They will let you know when you need to clear your energy field by their reactions. They're uncompromising and are not people pleasers, so you can trust their reaction as truth. Cats are honest and authentic luminaries, lighting the way for you to reveal your truest self.

Those drawn to learn from cats seek the 5D attributes of acceptance, authenticity, and emotional independence.

The Power of Purring

Scientists have demonstrated that cats purr during both inhalation and exhalation with a consistent pattern and frequency between 25 Hz and 150 Hz. Cat expert Professor Leslie A. Lyons, Ph.D., explains that frequencies between 20 Hz and 150 Hz are healing frequencies that can heal infections, decrease swelling and pain, induce muscle growth and repair, aid in tendon repair and joint mobility, and enhance bone density (which is why cats rarely have bone issues).

Your beloved cat companions are *literally* wired to heal you through their *purrfect* version of vibrational therapy.

We have likely all seen exceptions to the aforementioned species consciousness descriptions and had experiences with animals that exhibit atypical qualities for their species. For example, a cat that is codependent with their person or a dog that is emotionally detached. This is due to the animal's past life experiences as another species (more details in the pages to come) and the individualized soul contracts you have created with your animals, which significantly influence their behaviors and teachings to accommodate your shared growth agreements.

All domesticated animals are evolving at their own pace and contributing in the manner their Higher Self agreed to with their people, but they are *always* connected to the other animals within their species' stream of consciousness.

Raising Consciousness

If there is a particular species or breed of animal that brings up fear within you, or you think gets a bum rap, you can become a part of the greater solution by deliberately sending love to their breed or species consciousness. Several times in the past I was part of a group that sat in meditation together and sent love to the pit bull stream of energy to positively influence their collective vibration. There was so much fear and anger toward the breed that it had unintentionally affected the vibration of their stream of energy and contributed to their continued aggression. We have the ability to consciously choose our thoughts and actions from our minds and our hearts, so when you catch yourself in a negative thought, try to counterbalance it by sending positive energy to that species. This is a beautiful way to take responsibility for our thoughts, shift our fears, and serve a higher purpose that will have a positive ripple effect on many.

At any time, by yourself or with others, you can intentionally send love and gratitude to the consciousness of a particular animal species.

1. Bring your attention to your heart and take several deep breaths.
2. Ask for permission to connect to the stream of consciousness for the species of your choice or the animal kingdom as a whole.
3. Visualize a rainbow of light from your heart to the animal's field of consciousness.
4. Listen with your heart and sink into the connection. Feel their energy.
5. Send them love and gratitude for their teachings. They will feel it!

SOUL GROUPS AND REINCARNATION

One of the most fascinating things I've learned while facilitating healing sessions over more than twenty years is that there are frequently animals in our soul group! Our soul group, or *spiritual family*, is composed of beings that share a similar frequency that we collaborate with to grow and evolve. We share an intensely strong bond with each being within the soul group and have repeatedly incarnated together. All those in our soul group hold a deep mutual respect and love for each other. It is this strong soul familiarity that magnetizes us to each other once in our earthly bodies, and this includes our animal companions.

Your animal relationships are predestined and agreed upon prior to your arrival in your physical temple. Animal companions that you feel a deep heart connection and powerful bond with are usually in your extended soul group, and you have likely teamed up in many lives. This explains why you might feel an especially deep love connection with certain animals. We have undeniably shared long-standing histories with many animals.

You might observe that your companion exhibits a similar behavior or personality trait that they possessed in a past life to get your attention. They rarely show up as 100 percent of what they were like in their former life with you because we are all evolving, transforming, and choosing different experiences and lessons in each life. Most people just have a sense of familiarity about an animal and will mention that it reminds them of an animal that transitioned years prior.

The Comeback Healer
Denise & Cardog & Khusy

Cardog kitty was given her unique name because she loved sleeping on top of her mom's car, and, much like a dog, she'd enthusiastically run to greet her parents as if it had been a year since she'd last seen them. Denise, a counselor and holistic healer, had a profound and loving soul bond with Cardog that she deeply treasured. During the years they were together, Denise sometimes suffered from painful fibromyalgia. There were several times that she'd go to bed in extreme pain only to awaken and realize that she felt much better and the pain was completely gone. Then she'd zero in on the fact that her beloved cat Cardog was remarkably lying up against her back in the exact spot that had been the greatest source of her pain. Denise had been awakened each of those times by Cardog's purring motor set on the highest *healing* gear possible.

She recalls another similar incident of having a migraine and lying down to nap, only to awaken to the feeling of Cardog draped around the top of her head, purring loudly, and the migraine being no more. Cardog is undeniably a master healer and wayshower, and she was an essential source of support and healing for Denise for many years. Their relationship was the epitome of *who rescued who*. Cardog transitioned of old age just after the turn of the century.

Three years ago, Denise and her husband decided to look for another tabby cat to adopt because of their wonderful experience with Cardog. Upon arriving at the rescue center, they spotted a brown tabby with white socks and were immediately drawn to her kind and easygoing temperament. When Khusy rolled onto her back and invited Denise to rub her belly, that was it.

Much like Cardog, Khusy also has a noticeably loud purr with an easy on switch, and an insatiable appetite. But their personalities are uniquely different. Cardog was more of a people pleaser and loved being on her mom's lap all the time, while Khusy is more independent. In the years since Cardog passed, Denise no longer has fibromyalgia and migraines because she embarked on a deep inner healing journey that helped her heal the internal wounds that were contributing to the physical issues.

There have been a few times since bringing Khusy home that Denise wondered if she and Cardog were the same soul, but one evening two years ago she began thinking that possibility might be a reality.

Denise and her husband had just arrived home after traveling to attend a relative's funeral. She was tired and sat down to decompress from the event, which had taken its toll on them both. That's when out of the blue a long-time friend called to share that her husband had suddenly and unexpectedly passed away that evening. After they hung up, Denise began to cry so hard that she was having difficulty breathing. Magically, Khusy appeared as if out of thin air, ran into the room, and jumped up on Denise's lap. Purring at full throttle and staring deeply into her beloved mom's eyes, Khusy gently placed both of her front paws directly on Denise's breaking heart. After a few minutes of receiving Khusy's energy healing treatment, Denise began to feel much calmer, and her breathing normalized. With much gratitude, she looked into Khusy's soulful eyes and in that very moment sensed the undeniable familiarity between the two master healer cats.

A couple of times since then Khusy has carried out similar miraculous healings on Denise by lying on or touching the precise area of her body that needed healing, in the same exact manner as Cardog.

Cardog and Khusy most assuredly share the same soul. It is common for people and animal healing duos like Denise and Khusy to consciously collaborate to usher in a new Earth. These two lightworkers have more than likely been healers

Khusy

alongside each other in many lives. And the fact that Khusy is more independent now beautifully reflects the inner work that Denise has done to raise her vibration since Cardog left twenty years ago.

Both of my current cat companions, Bodhi and Rumi, have been with me before in *this* life. It's the third time for Rumi! I share their amazing reincarnation stories in *Animal Soul Contracts*. It was a wonderful and welcome surprise to learn through our heart connection that they are in my extended soul group. Even more, knowing that we share this sacred, intimate long-term connection comforts and soothes my soul. No matter what, our hearts will forever be connected, as will yours with your animal companions.

The important thing to take into account about your animals reincarnating to be with you again is to trust your Higher Self's plan as to if and when they come back to you in this life. Releasing control and trusting the process is helpful to you both, and it's also a very fifth-dimensional response to allow the timing to organically reveal itself.

FREE WILL

Sometimes while facilitating healing sessions, a past life of an animal client will reveal itself. Over the years, I've noticed that some animals have repeatedly incarnated as the same species of animal. More often, the animals have chosen a variety of different earthly animal bodies as host, likely to adapt to your mutual needs and preferences in a particular life in addition to your agreed upon soul contracts. For example, while you might be a dog person in this life, it is likely you partnered with a different species in a prior life.

It might be easy for you to recognize when your animals have had multiple past-life experiences as another type of species. From the moment that one of my prior cats, MaiTai, arrived in my home at three months of age, he sat up like a dog and waved his front paws together "begging" whenever he wanted something. From time to time, clients will casually share, for example, that their dog is more catlike, or their horse is more doglike. This is a sign that your animal has experienced lives in another type of animal body and retained the previous life's traits in their soul memory.

Animals have free will, as we do, and they can and will incarnate into different earthly vessels to have a variety of experiences. Being aware of this can raise your level of consciousness because it validates that at a soul level, each of us chooses our earthly experiences for our growth, even the ones with pain and suffering. Here's the great news: You can consciously begin shifting your life to have fewer insufferable 3D experiences by raising your frequency! This can occur as a result of doing your inner work, adopting 5D habits, and demonstrating compassion for *all* beings. The higher your frequency, the more spontaneous your loving intentions are to lift up others and be a bearer of hope and peace.

I recommend reading Robert Schwartz's book *Your Soul's Plan* for more information about how and why souls choose to create certain experiences for their growth. In addition, Part III of this book is dedicated to helping you raise your frequency, which will benefit not only yourself but also your wonderful animals and all others in your wake.

Rest assured that you and your animal are forever connected, and you will be with them again and again and again. With laser precision, your souls have intentionally planned every incarnation and every experience together to advance to higher dimensional living. Nothing can thwart your Divine destiny.

BEYOND THE PHYSICAL

The best and most beautiful things in the world cannot be seen or even touched—they must be felt with the heart.

HELEN KELLER

Is there anything better than receiving a heavenly visitation from a much-missed animal companion? There are endless ways your animals can drop in on you from the other side to confirm that your hearts are forever linked. They might come to you in a dream, or you might see their soul out of the corner of your eye or sense their essence when you need them. Many people have revealed that their animal companion will jump into a particular bird or butterfly to let them know they are thinking of them.

My friend Colleen and her husband sometimes hear their dog Gina bark from the other side; another friend shared that each of her family members have heard their dog Igor scratch on the front door, just like he used to when he was living with them. Every once in a while during meditation, my cat MaiTai, who passed several years ago, will pop into my cat Rumi and give me a beautiful slow blink. This was always one his favorite ways to express his love. Every fiber of my being knows it is unmistakably him.

The timing of these heavenly visits is always divinely coordinated to bring you peace, hope, or a desired lift and shift. Perhaps in that very moment you needed to lighten your mood, shift your thoughts, or get reconnected to spirit. Or maybe your heart was longing to release repressed emotions, and connecting to your companion on the other side was just the right antidote to bring about the desired healing release.

And yet there is much more to the continued relationship with our animals once they have transitioned back to spirit. While connected to animals in healing sessions during their actual transitions, they have sometimes shared that they are eager to leave their body so they can help their person more from the other side. So what exactly does that mean?

Typically, they remain actively engaged in your well-being,

and sometimes they have more freedom to help you without their body, especially if they were elder or had a lot of physical issues. Your hearts remain forever connected once they have returned to spirit, literally, through an energetic cord, so they always know what's up with you. Your animal will still be healing, guiding, and loving you from the other side, just as you would them if the tables were turned. You can officially think of them as being a part of your light team, available for you to call upon to bring you healing comfort. They will be there for you for deeper healing as well.

The Heavenly Healer
Anne & Mister

Spiritual intuitive Anne Peek realized just before her beloved cat Mister transitioned that he had been embodying the role of guardian angel for their entire family since the moment he arrived in the house. Mister would follow Anne and his two kitty sisters around the house, sitting at the thresholds as if he was standing guard, assuring them that he had their backs, all the while emanating a high-vibrational loving presence for each of them to lean into. Mister always had a playful and loving way about him that helped the entire family feel grounded, safe, and connected.

For some time after he passed in 2011, Anne frequently felt Mister's loving spirit around them. She always had the sense he was watching over his two grieving sisters and assuring them that he was still with them, just in a different way.

A couple of years ago I was facilitating a remote healing session on Anne while she laid on her sofa. Anne had diligently been clearing old, distorted beliefs and grief through our work together. During this particular session, Anne was feeling stuck, frustrated, and was heavily grieving because of longstanding physical pain. Suddenly Anne sensed the presence of Mister's spirit on top of the sofa, just over her right shoulder, radiating love. Then, with much purpose and intent, Mister specifically set his paw on the far-right side of Anne's chest. Immediately upon Mister's loving touch it was as if a dam burst, and Anne spontaneously released wave after wave of grief that had longed to be free. It was incredible, and she immediately felt better!

Mister's healing presence brought Anne so much comfort that day. Her profound love and respect for him deepened even more through his selfless actions to help her release the emotional pain. Mister is an animal wayshower. He remained with her for the duration of the session, then she felt him leave, having completed what he had set out to accomplish.

Mister

This is a wonderful example of how our animals are still helping us from the other side. Our healing partnerships continue once our animal kin have transitioned, and we will forever be joined and committed to helping each other evolve and ascend into the higher dimensions.

You can consciously connect with your animal at any time through the joining of your hearts. Trust that they hear your prayers and are actively in your life when you need them. Love is the fuel that maintains your connection.

Many times, we evolve *through* what we experience during and after our animal's passing. I have shared that my spiritual awakening went into hyperdrive once my cat Khalua passed. Her spirit returned that very evening and stayed with me for many months, helping me to navigate through a very difficult period of four losses. It was through her passing that her greatest teachings arrived, which exponentially raised my awareness. She was the guiding light that showed me the way to my heart's truest desires and a new path in life.

If your animal's passing has been difficult for you, ask their spirit to help you find the gifts of the experience, and perhaps that will begin the shift to seeing the higher purpose of their passing. Remember to lean into the abundance of spiritual support that is always available during challenging times.

Your animal companion angels are your spiritual sponsors on the other side. Our memories with them are forever imprinted on our hearts. With your conscious participation in your shared spiritual evolution, your animals can step up even more obviously to help you tackle any issue, even from the other side. They will forever love you and are wired to serve you!

5

Disaster Relief

Not all storms come to disrupt your life. Some come to clear your path.

UNKNOWN

DISASTERS AND STORMS

After the disastrous tsunami in 2004 that took more than ten thousand lives, H. D. Ratnayake, Deputy Director of Sri Lanka's Wildlife Department, said, "No elephants are dead, not even a dead hare or rabbit. I think animals can sense disaster. They have a sixth sense. They know when things are happening."

An hour prior to the disastrous event, elephants were seen running from the beach areas to higher ground. Flamingos suddenly left the low-lying wetlands, and at the national wildlife park, every animal was on the move seeking higher ground.

There are many theories about animals' sixth sense abilities. Their sense of smell and their hearing are much better than humans, which no doubt aids in their instinctively guided reactions. However, it is their ability to sense, feel, and see *energy* that most contributes to the magic we see in their actions. Everything is energy first. Every storm. Every disease. Every emotion.

We see evidence of "higher sense perception" more so in animals because of their ability to stay grounded to Mother Earth and connected to the Divine. In fact, they instinctively do whatever it takes to nurture and maintain those connections. Animals never question the validity that what they are sensing is real. They simply trust their intuition and respond accordingly. People, on the other hand, tend to have a more difficult time trusting themselves and their feelings.

In or around 2006, an F1 tornado landed about a quarter of a mile as the crow flies from my home. In the matter of one second, at exactly 3 a.m., I went from sound asleep to wide awake and sat up in my bed. Like the animals in Sri Lanka, I simply reacted and instinctively knew exactly what was happening. I heard the "roar of the train" that others have described hearing when a tornado is approaching, and I quickly went about trying to round up my cats, MaiTai and Sundance, and get them to our safe room, which was the walk-in master bedroom closet.

I just let out a big sigh even thinking about that process. Cat owners know there isn't a training manual in existence on how to herd cats in a crisis, because it's impossible. They feel the energy and take off. I was frantically running around the house, looking under beds, tables, and sofas, all to no avail. My beloved cats were nowhere to be found and the roar of the tornado was getting louder and louder.

Finally, I caved, said a prayer for them, and sought shelter in the closet. As I curled up on the floor in the corner of the closet, I suddenly felt a furry kitty beside me. I glimpsed under the low hanging clothes, and yup, there they both were, already in the safest place in the home. Now here's the thing: they *never* hung out in that closet. Nor was it a place they played, napped, or even occasionally wandered into. But there they were, hunkered down in the one room that didn't have windows.

I have reflected on that experience many times over. It serves to confirm what we know about animals' instincts and their ability to feel energy and respond accordingly. *My* spontaneous response to the storm and how quickly I awakened and went into action was also something I thought was interesting. The storm was a surprise. There wasn't a warning of potential tornadic weather prior to my going to bed that evening. I believe my sixth sense more easily kicked in because there wasn't an underlying stream of fear about the potentiality of the storm, and my mind was at peace, clearing up space to instinctively react in the present moment. Whatever the reason, it brought me peace to know that all three of us instinctively reacted accordingly.

You have the same ability to utilize your perfectly wired intuition. In general, most people are trained early in their lives to give away their power to others who are perceived to be more connected. We forget that we were born with the same intuitive endowments as animals. Over the first decade of our lives there typically isn't as much focus on how to mature emotionally through our feelings as there is with our intellect, which causes a disconnect in our capacity to believe, trust, and react on our feelings and intuition.

The first step in adhering to what the animals are so beautifully modeling for you is learning to trust yourself by strengthening your connection to a higher power, for example, through meditation. When you are more connected to the stream of higher consciousness, your intuition is naturally enhanced. In turn you will feel more connected to yourself as well as a higher power, which strengthens your capacity to trust yourself at a deeper level. Then, as you integrate these teachings, you will begin to notice the everyday synchronicities and small and large miracles that are certain to show up!

Because domesticated animals have a different type of role with people than animals in nature, their response to disasters and storms will differ according to their environment and soul mission. On the day of the tsunami in Sri Lanka, more dogs were seen running *toward* their homes and their people rather than trying to get to higher ground.

Upon choosing to team up with humans on this evolutionary journey, animals that live in our homes essentially have adapted their responses to natural disasters, because their soul mission is to partner with their people. If my cats had been living outside on their own at the time of the tornado, their instincts would have likely taken them in a completely different direction.

In the last few years, the west coast of the United States has unfortunately been engulfed in wildfires. On the first day of an online course I facilitated in 2020, I received an email from an attendee stating that she was being evacuated from her Oregon home due to the fires. She was having difficulty finding a way to get her horses to safety and feared she might have to leave them on their ranch. It is inconceivable to most animal lovers to think of leaving their animals to fend for themselves. Imagining any animal, let alone our beloved companions, suffering in any way is unthinkable.

With the attendee's permission, I shared with the group the reason she wasn't joining us that evening. When I observed that the vibration of the group had quickly dropped into fear for the horses' well-being, I invited them to close their eyes and participate in a meditation to help the horses. I suggested that everyone visualize the horses connecting with their innate sixth sense because it would surely guide them to safety. There is a release of the fear energy from the humans' side, which can assist in the process in these types of scenarios to free up the connection so the animals are steered solely by their internal guidance system to reach safety. Domesticated animals can feel when their people are in a heightened state of fear, and it affects them. Instinctively from a soul level, they'll want to alleviate their person's fear. Telling the animal, even telepathically, to listen to their innate sense to take care of themselves and that you will be fine is incredibly beneficial during situations like these.

✳   *Domesticated animals are always feeling their person's energy and responding to it.*

During the meditation, I invited the group to hold a vision for positive outcomes for the highest and best of all beings and to visualize spiritual support in the center of the situation so fear could be released, transformed, and new resources for better results could present themselves. The attendee was able to join us for the following week's class from the trailer she was then residing in, and she shared with the group that a place to take her horses to had miraculously been found and everyone was safe.

During the destructive Camp Fire in Paradise, California, in 2018, I read numerous stories about animals that had to be left at their homes as their person couldn't get to them. It was a fast and furious devastating fire that quickly burned through the entire city. The most challenging factor in this fire was that there was only one road in and out of the city. During interviews around the time of the fire, I was frequently asked to share my thoughts about how the fires affected the animals in nature or animals left behind. I always took the opportunity to remind people that animals have amazing instincts and that there was more than one road to safety for them. And to remember that there is always a Divine plan and a surge of spiritual support guiding all beings through disasters.

There were several stories of those that arrived home afterward to dogs that were haggard, tired, and covered with burns, and yet they could see that the dogs had never stopped herding the other animals on the property, like horses, sheep, and so on. It was simply incredible hearing how those amazing dogs had stayed in their role of keeping the other animals safe. They are truly wayshowers.

I've prepared some tips for you to have in your emergency tool bag, should you ever need them. (Hoping you don't!)

Tips for Emergencies with Your Animals

- Create a plan in advance of an unexpected storm or emergency. This will aid in your ability to quickly react and stay grounded in the present moment, versus being immobilized and disempowered by fear. Plan out what you'll do with your animals, and store their crates in an easy-to-grab place.
- Call upon help from the heavens. Don't be shy! Ask for help from who you feel most connected with on the other side. You can ask a legion of angels for support,

or Archangel Uriel, who resides over animals and earthly creatures. Or the fairy realm and Saint Francis. I highly suggest calling on the help from these beings in emergencies, small or large. Trust that help is immediately granted.

- Remind yourself that you are never alone, and there is a Divine plan. Take deep breaths and stay in your body. Your animals always respond to *your* energy so "put your oxygen mask on first" applies whenever you fear for their well-being.
- Team up with your animals to instinctively navigate through the crisis period. Depending on the situation, they might know a way out that is safer for you both.
- As soon as you can, move out of your fear with the intention of keeping your power. This will enable you to help others affected by the same event. Your animals beautifully model this 5D behavior and you can emulate their teachings. Plus, helping other beings is one of the fastest ways to be and feel supported, safe, empowered, and loved.
- Seek the gifts of the experience as soon as you can, and express gratitude for the blessings bestowed upon you and your animals.

HEALING DURING THE COVID-19 PANDEMIC

The Feline Caretaker
Donna & Eiryk

It was the first class of my January 2021 online masterclass course titled Healing the Emotional Wounds of Animals. As attendees shared a little about themselves, I couldn't help but notice that one of the participants that I'd worked with previously, an end-of-life mobile veterinarian, was lying in bed under the covers. During her introduction, she explained that she had contracted COVID-19 and would be trying her best to listen to the class but would not be actively participating until she felt better. At this point of the pandemic, knowing someone that had the virus was more common, but you could still feel the empathy and concern from all in the group when Donna shared her diagnosis.

Prior to the second week's class, Donna reached out to share a remarkable story about her cat, Eiryk. I knew from working with her that she had a deep soul bond with Eiryk. Their love story began while she was working at an animal clinic prior to opening her private practice. One day someone dropped off a cat with a respiratory infection to be treated; after a week the clinic personnel came to realize the person had no intention of returning to retrieve Eiryk and likely had intentionally abandoned

Eiryk

him. After all attempts to reunite Eiryk with his person were unsuccessful, Donna went over to his kennel and picked him up, and he literally wrapped his front legs around her neck in a loving embrace. He went home with her that day, and she has never looked back.

From the onset of Donna's illness, Eiryk lay on her bed nonstop, only leaving to eat or use the litter box and then quickly resuming his position. Donna's fever then spiked and would not break. By day three of having a consistently high fever, Donna felt miserable and was very frightened. That's when Eiryk suddenly got more persistent. He adamantly insisted upon getting under the covers and curling up in the nook of Donna's torso as she lay on her side. After a bit he vomited a phlegmy substance. Then he jumped onto the floor and vomited a lot of fluid. Moments later, Donna's fever "miraculously" broke. Eiryk's behavior then shifted and he casually went back to his regular routine in the house prior to his mom contracting the virus.

The pandemic of 2020–2021 unearthed a new time in history, and it affected almost every being on the planet. As I'm writing this in the first half of 2021, there is uncertainty as to exactly how long the remnants of the virus will linger. The vaccines have arrived and are being distributed en masse, which has greatly contributed to ushering in more peace.

From the moment the announcements about the potential quarantine time began, I had complete clarity about my role. With laser focus I proclaimed to the universe that I wanted to serve those that my healing skill set could benefit. Those who know me well are familiar that sometimes it takes me a minute or two to find clarity, but when things come through so distinctly, as they did at that time, I make it a point to follow my guidance and take the appropriate action.

What's interesting is that six months *prior* to the pandemic quarantine period in the United States, after years of resistance, I decided to begin facilitating my classes exclusively online. Beginning in January 2020 I unexpectedly had a new landlord for my office rental, and even though we had discussed it, somehow we never signed a lease. When I reached out to her a couple of weeks into quarantine about no longer needing the office because my practice was shifting to 100 percent virtual, she seemed relieved. Unbeknownst to me she wanted to use my office to expand her chiropractic practice. And to top it off, she purchased much of my office furniture that I no longer needed. *And*, two months prior to the shutdowns, I suddenly felt guided to purify and cleanse my physical temple. I took caffeine, gluten, dairy, and (almost all) sugar out of my diet.

As I reflect on the synchronicities I experienced during those months, undoubtedly it seems as if my soul was getting in alignment to serve those that were negatively affected by the pandemic. During the sessions I facilitated in the throes of the highest emotional time, I was consistently aware of a new level of service that our animal companions had seemingly been preparing for as well. Time and time again I noticed that animals were more actively participating in their person's healing session. It was fascinating!

I've often noticed the souls of animals assisting their person's healing sessions, even if the animal had previously transitioned, but there was something different in their energy during the pandemic. I perceived a heightened sense of intentionality and purpose. It was like the difference between a doctor preparing to perform a routine surgery and an emergency room doctor gearing up to simultaneously treat multiple trauma victims.

One of the most significant "gifts" of the pandemic (and there are always gifts that arrive with momentous events) was the golden opportunity for us to take deeper dives into our personal growth. From the moment we were instructed to quarantine, everyone's lives were changed in substantial ways. In general, people don't necessarily lean into new ways and habits with the greatest of ease. Most of us understandably long to keep the status quo in our lives to feel safe and comfortable. We trust what we know and what we've been conditioned to believe to be true. Early in the pandemic we didn't know what to expect or even if we'd have enough of the fundamental needs like food and water, which catapulted most people into elevated levels of fear.

During the first few months, primal survival fears were rampant, which further served to exacerbate feelings of being out of control, which triggered unresolved emotional wounds, traumas, and even past-life issues. Many lost their jobs, and too many companies were forced to close their doors. Financial fears were very prevalent, along with the fear of possibly losing a loved one, especially an elder, to the virus.

Due to new restrictions, we were unable to be present with loved ones in hospitals, assisted living facilities, and veterinary clinics to provide comfort during difficult times and sometimes during their final moments. This was one of the most prevalent fears that triggered a great deal of distress. The separation component of the pandemic went against primal human needs and desires to be with those we care about to feel loved, nourished, and connected. Everyone was starving for the nurturing love of friends and family and the release of dopamine and oxytocin derived from hugs and loving touch.

Enter the frontline warriors of the animal kingdom, our beloved animal companions, who showed up with open hearts, willing and ready to serve their people and help them through whatever emotions had surfaced. Your animal companions are wired to help you feel better . . . and they can *always* feel your vibrational changes and shifts. Unquestionably, they were tapping into the underlying stream of fear that was suddenly present in their beloved people, and they instinctively stepped up their level of service. Dr. Donna's extraordinary experience with her cat Eiryk is a perfect example of what animals can and will do to help their humans.

An Explosion of Grief

While facilitating sessions during the first couple of months of the pandemic, it became abundantly clear that both two-legged *and* four-legged clients were releasing bucketfuls of repressed grief. The common theme in almost all sessions was the release of grief, and/or they were having a physical issue with their lungs.

Once contracted, the COVID-19 virus typically beelines to the lungs, which was the underlying issue in most of the virus deaths. In general, our lungs are weakened by repressed and unreleased sadness and grief. If a person's lungs were compromised by suppressed grief and sadness *prior* to contracting the virus, there was a greater chance of them being negatively affected. More than any other time that I can recall, I had more clients—two-legged and four-legged—with lung issues, and that's when I realized there was clearly a collective healing opportunity to move out deep levels of grief and sadness.

Highly sensitive empathic people, a group that frequently overlaps with animal lovers, were especially feeling the waves of grief and sadness that were "up" for clearing in the collective. It became normal for many lightworkers to spontaneously cry without knowing the cause of the sudden onset of the release. Lightworker animals and people everywhere were unconsciously or consciously aiding in the clearing of deep-seated grief that was given a perfect storm scenario opportunity to release. This transpired for myself several times a week for months, and many of my peers shared similar stories of sudden bouts of crying.

I see this phenomenon to collectively release repressed grief as being spirit guided to aid in humanity's reaction to the virus and to lighten the emotional load to enhance and strengthen the health of our lungs. Given that more people were at home, it was easier to lean in to the healing energy available to release emotions that perhaps might still be repressed if the pandemic had never occurred.

Our animal companions were also actively participating in moving out their grief, their person's repressed grief, and aiding in the collective purification of our lungs.

✳ *If we aspire to see the higher purpose in every experience, we are sure to find extraordinary opportunities for healing and growth.*

Animals have always played a significant role in the emotional well-being of humanity in unprecedented times. They have the ability to help us navigate isolation by feeling loved and connected to other beings. They are experts on both subjects and model a way of being that we humans can strive to emulate.

Repeatedly, during those initial months of the pandemic, clients shared that their animals were suddenly more affectionate than ever before. Make no mistake, your animals were undoubtedly thrilled that you were home more often, and their higher purpose actions remained laser sharp to respond to your new needs. They were (and are) determined and dedicated allies ready to help us feel better and assist in any deep soul-nudging transformational shifts that arrived with that unprecedented time.

My cat companions Bodhi and Rumi were especially attentive and provided much-needed solace during those crucial first few months of adapting to the change of living a more solitary lifestyle. When I had even a fleeting thought about how much I missed hugging my family and friends, a kitty would appear seemingly out of nowhere and jump on my lap, ready to serve. Sometimes in those loving moments with Bodhi or Rumi, tears would gently roll down my cheeks. Their unconditional love unfailingly shifted me from fear and loneliness to feeling loved and connected, which induced a beautiful release. Then I'd find myself naturally taking deeper breaths and reconnecting to my heart and remembering with utmost certainty that I am never alone.

Domesticated animals are instinctively aware of the essential need for touch, for them and for you. Most everyone was sorely missing being with and physically touching those they care about. Animals are masters at providing loving touch and most are not shy about asking for it in return because they have similar needs. *All* mammals are sentient beings and have a version of oxytocin that is released during loving encounters. If you believe their enhanced level of affection is self-serving,

I propose that you look at the higher perspective in those moments and tap into your needs to see how they just might have been tending to *your* well-being.

Welcome Relief
Sami & Adjiti

Sami lives in spiritual Bali, where open doors are common and domesticated animals are free to create their own schedules and choose their families. At the onset of the pandemic in March of 2020, Adjiti the kitty had been living with a couple next door to Sami when she abruptly adjusted her sails and became quite determined to live with Sami. It didn't take long at all for Sami to fall in love with the adorable, affectionate cat. She enjoyed having her companionship and recognized it as a loving soul partnership that she welcomed.

Soon after Adjiti moved in, Sami experienced an abundance of emotional and physical stress that arrived during the pandemic time. She self-isolated for several weeks and then unfortunately had a severe neck pull that required ten days of bedrest. Adjiti was always close by ministering to her. In Sami's darkest moments, Adjiti would rest her head on Sami's heart to lovingly console her and provide healing energy. Once when Sami had a nightmare, she was intentionally awakened by her beloved companion. Adjiti jumped up and sat on top of Sami's heart and meowed until she woke up.

A few months later, they moved to a new house. Adjiti effortlessly adapted to the new surroundings and quickly developed a new routine. Every day at sunrise Adjiti left to go visit a nearby temple where she would hold space for others all day, but she always returned home promptly at sunset.

Then in the middle of October during the noon hour, Sami's mum unexpectedly passed away. Within twenty minutes of receiving the phone call with the dire news, Adjiti suddenly showed up, out of her normal routine, and ran into the house meowing incessantly. Sami said that it was as if Adjiti was exclaiming, "It's okay, I'm here." The wayshower cat then jumped onto Sami's lap and leaned into her sacred work of comforting and serving her beloved person through a big transitional period in her life.

The timing of Adjiti's arrival into Sami's life at the onset of the pandemic was no coincidence. Adjiti's sensitive and intuitive soul was enacting a purposeful mission of service. At a soul level, they designed for their lives to interact such that Adjiti could provide the loving care Sami needed. She is a master healer and the two of them were destined to be together. Their healing partnership has been mutually beneficial, as

Adjiti

Sami's love has also provided profound healing for beloved Adjiti. The name Adjiti is derived from the Sanskrit name of the goddess *Aditi,* the mother of all mothers, the goddess of earth, sky, unconsciousness, the past, and the future. It's the perfect name for this nurturing luminary cat.

Forever Serving
Ricia & Maddie

Throughout the first year of the pandemic, sometimes animals stepped up to serve their people, only to transition after their loving service work was completed. When Ricia and Roston both contracted COVID-19 in September of 2020, their dearly loved dog Maddie became their caretaker and refused to leave their sides until they were both over the worst of the symptoms. Maddie was elderly and had several physical issues that were being monitored prior to her human parents coming down with the virus, but she'd been doing okay.

After several weeks, when Ricia and Roston were well on the road to recovery, they suddenly noticed that Maddie wasn't doing well and was in fact getting worse each day. Since they were still honoring the appropriate quarantine time, they contacted their vet tech son who quickly took her in to be checked out by his vet. Unfortunately, the results were ominous.

That's when they realized that Maddie's soul had intentionally decided to stay in her body long enough to help them heal from the virus. Maddie had always tended to her family's physical well-being, especially Roston, through many challenges. Maddie's physical ailments frequently mirrored the ailments of her parents, which indicates that she was helping them to heal by absorbing the energy of their illnesses. Ricia

Maddie

believes that Maddie stuck around for one last healing gig on their behalf, and, ultimately, it had contributed to her physical temple's departure, as part of a higher plan.

It is extraordinary and quite noble of Maddie to serve her parents for the duration of time they were ill before revealing that her physical temple was ready to be released. Maddie is a wayshower and was always vibrationally tuned in to the higher needs of their family. Weeks after their recovery from COVID-19, the family lovingly assisted Maddie's transition back to spirit.

Be assured that your animal companions consciously and intentionally aligned with your needs during the pandemic. During the 2020–2021 pandemic, they connected to a higher frequency of healing energy to support your transformational soul healing and ease the flux of emotions that arose from humanity's reactions and triggers.

✳   *Your lightworker animal companions are the first*
responders, nurturers, healers, and companions.

Remember that our souls are always creating experiences that will catapult our growth to the next level. *Taking advantage of the expedited soul growth that is available during historic events is a very conscious choice.* Humanity will get through this time and more. Your feelings are a guiding light to take you deeper into your evolutionary journey. How you react to them is where the growth begins. Look to your animals for guidance. They are more regularly tapped into a higher level of consciousness and will, like a lighthouse, *show you the way* back to your heart.

Seek the gifts held in the heart of your pandemic experience. When you shift your perspective to look for the gifts, your vibration immediately increases and, in turn, this opens the window to allow in more support from your animals and the universe. It moves you from 3D to 5D.

One of the most fabulous gifts that came about *because* of the pandemic were the thousands upon thousands of animals that were adopted and found their forever homes. At the onset of the pandemic, animal rescue shelters had to discontinue in-person adoptions, and the animals were put into foster homes. There were a record number of "foster failures," meaning the foster parent ended up adopting the animal, in addition to the fact that it was the perfect time to integrate a new animal into the family due to the number of people working from home. Even more sought out the companionship and love of an animal to ease the discomfort of living a more introverted, independent lifestyle. Many shelters declared that every single animal was adopted, and they were able to then save the lives of even more animal wayshowers!

Take a few minutes to write down the gifts and blessings you received during the pandemic. This process will aid in your journey to feeling more empowered and to seeing the light held within your pandemic experience. Close out this exercise by expressing gratitude for the growth opportunities and other treasures you received during this tumultuous, unprecedented period.

Your animal kin are your healers and copilots helping you to navigate through the unexpected disasters, storms, and pandemics that arrive on your doorstep. You can trust yourself and the heart connection you share with your animal to guide you through each life storm, knowing that everything is unfolding in your highest good. No matter how much fear is up for you in any given moment, you can trust that there is a spiritual support reaching out to console you that you can lean into . . . and it might just arrive through a paw.

Rumi meditating with Tammy

PART II

The Sacred Partnership

The highest purpose of a relationship is to elevate the collective consciousness by amplifying the vibration of unconditional love.

ISABEL MARIA

6

The Divine Collaboration

*In the long history of humankind (and animal
kind, too) those who learned to collaborate and
improvise most effectively have prevailed.*

CHARLES DARWIN

Years ago I read about the "Hearts Aligned" study con-
ducted in 2016 at Melbourne Monash University in
Australia. Researchers placed heart rate monitors on several
dogs and their owners. Then they separated the dogs from
their humans, documented their heart rates, then reunited
the pairings and checked them again. As you might expect,
the heart rates of the people and the dogs instantly dropped
once they were brought back together. What they *didn't*
expect was that the heart rate patterns of the dog and their
person would actually sync and mirror each other. Indeed,
within every pairing, the dogs breathing patterns began falling and rising in complete synchronicity with their person
when they were reunited.*

The HeartMath Institute performed a similar study,

---

*See the article by Sue Dunlevy, "Bond between Man and Dog Is Closer
Than You Thought—How Canines Hearts Are in Sync with Ours" on the
news.com.au website.

which showed the exact same results. The results demonstrated that there is biomagnetic communication between people and animals.*

These fascinating studies validate and confirm what animal lovers are already aware of—that our energy merges with our dearly loved animals because of our incredible spiritual connection. Biomagnetic communication transpires between spiritual partners that have a relationship grounded in the purity of unconditional love. The studies are a perfect symbolic representation of what happens when two beings who are bonded by sacred soul contracts come together.

Each animal-human pairing is literally a match made in heaven. Actually, the animals we share our lives with are predestined *by our souls* for our mutual growth. I never tire of hearing how animals and people come together. More often than not, there is an unmistakable soul recognition upon finding each other again. One of my favorite stories of two beings reuniting is about a writer, Sally, and her beloved cat Tamsin.

The Heart Knows
Sally & Tamsin

Unfortunately, 2019 was a year that Sally wishes had never arrived. Her husband of twenty-nine years, Sandy, unexpectedly passed from a brainstem aneurysm that May. Several months later, Laurence, Sally's beloved guide dog, retired from guide work and went to live with family friends in Florida. Sally has been legally blind for two decades and deaf in both ears for eight years due to an age-related genetic hearing loss.

---

*See "A Boy and His Dog—Heart-Rhythm Entrainment" on the HeartMath website.

Suddenly Sally was utterly and completely alone. While she had learned to adapt to the challenges of not having her sight, losing the external guidance from the two beings that knew and loved her the most was extremely difficult. Her heart was broken, and every day seemed to arrive with more loneliness and less mobility. Sally and her husband never had children, and she didn't have any relatives that lived nearby, so there wasn't a back-up support system to bridge her through that period of her life to becoming more independent.

The holidays were nearing and one thing was crystal clear, Sally knew she didn't want to be alone during that holy time of year. So she did the only logical thing she could think of: she asked a friend to take her to a local no-kill shelter and let a cat rescue her.

From the moment they brought Tamsin into the meet-and-greet-room with Sally and her friend, the beautiful cat only had eyes for Sally—it was as if she had finally found the long-lost friend she'd been searching for. Tamsin had been turned in to the shelter three months prior as a stray with a litter of kittens. As you can imagine, all the kittens were quickly adopted, leaving Tamsin all alone with no family to take care of and no one to love. Sally had a wonderful feeling about the affectionate cat from the moment they met. It was a perfect match. She signed the papers right then and there.

Sally's assumption that her new cat companion would hide under the sofa for days on end—was quickly proved wrong. What are the odds that within an hour of arriving in her new home, Tamsin would have found and used the litter box, eaten dinner, played with the new toys on the floor, and then found the blanket Sally had intentionally left on the sofa for her? When Tamsin lay down on that blanket and relaxed into a catnap, Sally's heart smiled for the first time in a very long time. She curled up on Sally's bed that very first night, as if she'd lived there all of her life. Furthermore, Tamsin, much like a dog, has always responded to her name and comes to Sally when called, as if she intuitively knows that her mom needs her to respond in this way.

Tamsin was by far the most miraculous gift Sally received that year, and she continues to bring her mom much comfort. It blows my mind to think about the how the universe magically orchestrates bringing together those that are destined to be in a relationship. It's as if the two beings that are meant to be together will be energetically magnetized to each other. When we trust that everything that happens to us is working for our highest and best, the miracles that arrive with those we are to know and love find their way to us more easily. Sally beautifully followed her internal guidance to connect with Tamsin and usher

Tamsin

in a mutually beneficial and well-deserved divine collaboration of the heart.

Our animal companions have the remarkable ability to bring purity, grace, and light to any discord within us. Embarking on a divine collaboration *with* our animal companions helps us to cultivate organic inner transformation as we move through the resistance keeping us from living more fully in the present moment. Yes, consciously partnering with these amazing luminaries will foster clarity, confidence, spontaneity, and joy in our lives. Indeed, there are endless benefits for animal lovers who are awakened to their animals' infinite gifts.

As an animal lover, you probably already know firsthand that domesticated animals are wired with natural healing abilities and intuitively know exactly what you need in any given moment. Some of this is due to their ability to feel and read your energy, including the emotions you have repressed into your subconscious. Your energy always tips them off as to the emotions you need to release that are contributing to the manifestation of 3D physical issues and undesired experiences. When you undergo a more conscious relationship with your animal companions, you will both feel better and have fewer ailments, frustrations, negative habits, and unwanted patterns.

Since my mid-twenties, I've partnered with numerous cats for my personal growth. However, in those early years, my beautiful felines were really working overtime because I was completely unconscious to their teachings. Once I awakened to the fact that my cats and I are copilots on the same flight to a higher dimension, *everything* changed for the better. My connection with my current cat companions,

Bodhi and Rumi, is much lighter and healthier. With much gratitude, I am no longer dependent on my animal companions to feel loved and know that I am lovable. This transformation didn't happen overnight, but it was so worth it to take a deeper dive into these life-changing relationships to receive their healing gifts and teachings.

I realize that I am not alone with relying pretty heavily on animals for many years of my life. This deep-seated emotional reliance and codependency on animals generally transpires with those who have learned, consciously or unconsciously, that people aren't as safe to be around as animals. Your soul ingeniously signed up to engage in sacred partnerships with animals to fill the hole in your heart and allow their love to heal and transform you. And know that it is okay that you have leaned on them. They would never want you to take this knowing and turn it against yourself. On the contrary, they are hoping for just the opposite outcome, which is the way you can best honor their courageous work—by knowing that every single part of you is deserving of *your* love.

Many animals are hoping their person has a breakthrough and turns a corner to become aware that you are Divine collaborators with spiritual work to do together in the fourth or fifth dimension. Their intention is to aid in your ascension to the higher dimensions, which sometimes means helping you to release repressed emotions by triggering you into those emotions through an unwanted behavior. Collaborating with the intention to evolve together will greatly enhance your sense of self and your ability to discover and reveal your authentic self. And remember that receiving and giving go hand in hand when collaborating.

Throughout Part II of the book, you'll come to learn numerous ways that people have consciously aligned with their lightworker animal companions to cocreate, receive and reveal more light, and shift to a higher frequency. These intimate stories just might bring a new level of awareness and insights into *your* divine animal collaborations.

The following examples reveal the higher purpose of two extraordinary animal light warriors who are guiding lights for their person to break through the protection around their hearts and move to a new level of consciousness with their companions.

The Awakening
Kathy & Murray

Out of all of the adoptable bunnies, Kathy zeroed in on Murray from the moment she laid eyes on him—he resembled her beloved bunny Smokey, who had just transitioned weeks before. Even though Murray came as part of a package deal with his two companions, Frankie and Goldie, Kathy's good nature was willing to bring them all home and provide all three bunnies with a good life.

After Murray moved into his new forever home, he continued to nestle deeper into his mom's heart in a way no other being had done before him. Even though he had difficulty trusting his mom, there was an undeniable deep soul connection between them that forged new ground in Kathy's heart. Murray's unconditional love began changing her from that very first day.

He wasn't the first mini-lop bunny she had taken in, but he was the first one that had an abundance of chronic physical manifestations from the onset of its arrival. Murray had a plethora of GI issues, dental issues, ear infections, thyroid issues, and then, toward the end, an enlarged heart. Kathy felt as if she was constantly on high alert, dealing with one ailment after another.

Given the fact that their connection was so strong, Kathy often spent her time worrying about his well-being and was determined to do whatever she could to get his sensitive body feeling better. It was as if they were constantly at veterinarian or animal specialists' offices. Unfailingly upon leaving, Kathy would feel frustrated because the traditional medications and well-intended veterinarian guidance that they were stringently following wasn't resolving Murray's ailments.

This led Kathy to begin taking matters into her own hands, which was new behavior for her because she'd always been one to strictly follow the guidance of doctors. She began looking into holistic modalities for the first time in her life. Because of her deep love for Murray, she was willing to try anything so her beloved bunny would have less suffering and, in turn, a better quality of life.

Kathy partnered with an animal communicator for help with his physical issues, which served to further enlighten her to Murray's higher purpose teachings in her life. She discovered that she and Murray had trust issues they were resolving together. Around that time, Kathy miraculously began hearing Murray speak to her telepathically, guiding her as to his wishes and preferences. At first she was in disbelief, but after a while she began to trust her new intuitive connection with Murray as truth. This newfound skill stirred up childhood memories of having this ability to communicate with animals when she was young. Alas, it was not understood nor accepted by her mother, so Kathy pushed her psychic gift into her subconscious.

All along, Murray's soul mission had been to catapult
Kathy into a spiritual awakening, and to support her in trusting
her intuition and feeling empowered to discern what is right
for herself and for the animals under her care. Murray then
began expressing external validation that things were coming
together just as their souls had planned. After three years, she

Kathy and Murray (receiving an acupuncture treatment)

received her very first bunny kiss from him, which continued daily until he passed, and she never once took them for granted. Murray outlived both of his companions due to Kathy learning how to instinctively read his sensitive body's needs and receive his messages. While Kathy had always selflessly nurtured her pets, Murray was the first animal companion who opened her heart and raised her awareness to the realization that all beings are created equal.

Kathy sometimes senses Murray's presence, or he pops in during a tandem healing session I'm facilitating with Kathy and one of her current bunnies, Buxton. Murray is still actively engaged in supporting Kathy's ascension journey and reminding her that she is never alone and is powerful beyond measure. Murray is a lightworker and is one of Kathy's greatest teachers in this life, and feeling his soul reassures her that they will forever be joined through their hearts.

Mirror Mirror
Susan & Ojas

Susan Petschauer has experienced more than her fair share of abuse and trauma in her life. Unfortunately, she suffered invasiveness, abandonment, and betrayal many times over throughout her childhood. Once out on her own, Susan's top coping mechanism to feel safe has been to control everything in her life to assure it is perfect in hopes of keeping "bad" experiences at bay. She was very young, too young, when she acquired the role of the responsible one in her family. Because of this, she developed into a hypervigilant caretaker and protector of those she loves in an attempt to minimize any and all pain . . . theirs and hers.

Four years ago, Susan and her husband decided a dog

companion would be the perfect addition for their young family. From the instant Susan set eyes on Ojas everything about her strategy to control her world began to unravel—perhaps a better term would be *transform*.

Ojas had the key to unlock Susan's heart, and he used it on that very first day. Susan was more than smitten; she was over the moon in love with the adorable puppy. Without hesitation, Susan donned her "responsible one" supermom cape with sights set on protecting her beloved Ojas from everything. Alas, her beautiful and loving intentions were not able to prevent their sacred soul contracts from revealing themselves.

Ojas had always exhibited some anxiety, but it was an experience with a veterinarian when he was fourteen months old that completely shifted his behavior. During that visit, he received four vaccinations, and two of them regrettably hit a bone. Ojas screamed, vomited, and cried in pain all night. After that experience, Ojas became fear reactive and would growl and snap at anything he perceived as potentially invasive, which included groomers, veterinarians, and children.

His new trust issue reactions, along with his many digestive, liver, and elimination issues, kept momma caretaker working overtime to find a way for her beloved dog to heal and feel better. Each and every day, Susan was in full-on panic mode, constantly monitoring him, filled with anxiety and worry, and nothing seemed to be shifting for the better. It was about this time that Susan's husband gifted her my first book, *Soul Healing with Our Animal Companions*. When Susan reached out to schedule sessions, her focus at that point was entirely on getting Ojas feeling better in the hope that this would bring them both more peace. But the direction of Susan's course of action was about to change!

Since her twenties, Susan has been riddled with "mystery" physical symptoms that have baffled many doctors, with indications of something awry within her liver and digestive system. She's also always had a lot of anxiety, and at one point she had a very invasive and traumatic experience with a doctor, which instantaneously created trust issues.

Soon after the first healing session, Susan's level of awareness shifted, and suddenly she could clearly see the mirroring between herself and Ojas. With much eagerness, she then courageously embarked on a deep transformational journey with Ojas to heal their mirroring physical issues and the core emotional wounding that created them. Susan became a student to these new spiritual teachings and had utmost clarity that Ojas is not only her mirror but her advocate and guide, helping her to peel back the layers of protection created by her childhood abuse and traumas. She also saw the parallels in their trust issues and learned that she must release the need to control everything because not only was it an impossible undertaking, it was holding herself and those she loved back from doing their own inner work.

Susan also realized that she'd been neglecting her own self-care by worrying about Ojas and everyone else. She got in touch with her emotions and gave herself permission to cry, grieve, and release decades of pain. She dove headfirst into researching and embracing alternative healing modalities, herbs, and supplements, because she understood that their sensitive systems responded better to those.

Nowadays they meditate together twice daily, and when Susan cries and releases, Ojas calmly lies next to her, holding Transformational Healing Presence. In typical wayshower fashion, Ojas doesn't coddle her during her releases, he simply sighs and breathes into the release with her. This has helped them both tremendously.

Much like a cosmic two-by-four, Ojas arrived in Susan's life to lovingly jolt her out of her comfort zone, raise her awareness, and support her in releasing the protection around her heart to feel safe enough to release the emotional pain of her past. Because of Ojas coming into her life, Susan has been studying animal acupressure, traditional Chinese medicine, and animal massage therapy to help animals and their people heal through utilizing less invasive alternative modalities.

More importantly, through their shared inner healing journey, Susan awakened to the importance of loving and treating herself with the same amount of love, compassion, and forgiveness that she freely gives to countless others. She now looks at Ojas's behavior and physical issues as the barometer for which she measures what is happening within herself. Susan expresses gratitude daily for the transformation and gifts that originated through their sacred soul partnership.

These two courageous light warriors harmoniously came together to transform their pain into love and to raise the collective consciousness, beginning with lightening their (emotional) load, raising their vibration, and helping others to do the same.

✳ *The animal companions in your life are your personal ascension guides, showing you the way to fulfill your destiny.*

The Higher Selves of you and your animals have intentionally teamed up and are orchestrating your experiences for your highest and best. Together there is a warm and loving resonance that unfolds. As we consciously connect with our

Ojas and Susan

animal companions, they become beacons of universal energy and light within us, igniting the soul memories that link us back to our spiritual families and catapult us into a higher frequency. In the remembering of our soul connection within the collective consciousness, animals then embody the role of a spiritual compass, guiding us back to our sacred role in raising the vibration for ourselves, them, and the collective. Our souls are beautifully and infinitely intertwined.

Journal or reflect on how your animal has positively influenced your level of awareness. Breathe into your heart and seek to observe your relationship from a higher perspective.

Take note of the times that there was an experience with your animal that catapulted you into a different direction to learn something new or look at something differently.

7

Transformational Deep Dives

We delight in the beauty of the butterfly, but
rarely admit the changes it has gone through to
achieve that beauty.

MAYA ANGELOU

More than ever before it seems as if people who are awakened to a spiritual path are drawn to animals for their sage teachings. Many are utilizing the healing offerings of their animal companions by embarking on a deep shadow transformational journey alongside them to reveal more of their inner light and automatically gravitate to 5D living. We are often more receptive to working on healing our "stuff" with animals because we know their spirit is pure, and the only agenda they have is *ours*.

One of your animals' goals is to motivate you to look within and begin parenting yourself in healthy ways that you might not have been exposed to early in your life. Early developmental trauma and unresolved emotional wounds will continue to show up in your life until you set up the internal and external support to know that it is safe to dive deeper into the emotions and wounds that long to be free. Internal parenting requires that you have compassion and forgiveness for yourself for all that you have lived through. Compassion and forgiveness are high vibrational pinnacle teachings that our animals have mastered. Their ability to exquisitely convey these essential 5D attributes with ease and grace shows us the way to do the same for ourselves and other beings.

When you team up with your animal kin on a transformational deep dive, they have the ability to hold the exact vibration needed to bring about the growth your soul desires. Too many times to count, I've seen an animal's negative behavior turn on a dime when their person receives the higher purpose message their animal is diligently conveying to them through a behavior or physical issue, or even through their dreams or telepathy.

The "louder" their negative behavior, and the more emotionally triggered you are by it, the more important the message is for your growth. They are willing to be your mirror of love or an unwelcome button pusher, whichever works best to shift your awareness to the part of you that needs *your* love and attention. Their willingness to do this for you reflects the depth of their avid devotion and commitment to your personal growth. Your animals are often beckoning you to go even deeper into the core wounds that are behind both of your unwanted patterns, addictions, behaviors, and physical issues. Know that these deep dives are well worth your attention, and you will be aptly rewarded with feeling more love and joy more often.

⁂ *When you intentionally choose to embark upon a transformational healing journey with your animals, the deeper, more profound soul healing work will organically progress and bring you both the well-deserved peace you seek. You will both significantly benefit from your meaningful mission to heal together.*

The following stories are of two remarkable people and their lightworker animals that were brave enough to dip their toes in the waters of transformation. Subsequently, this led them to experience incredibly healing soul purifications with their animals, which might just inspire you to do the same.

As you read each story, empower it to gift you with a teaching in your highest and best. Following each story are writing prompts and exercises to assist you in activating or deepening your soul partnership with your animal kin.

Jumping Hurdles of the Heart
Stephanie & Unicum

Unicum is a strikingly handsome Belgian Warmblood born to a breeder in a small village in Maaseik, near the Dutch border. Stephanie felt a deep kinship with Unicum even before she met him. She saw his photo on an announcement seeking someone to split the three-year-old's care and livery costs. She was torn because it wasn't a great time to take on the laborious care of a horse. She was young, and anticipated moving soon, but her heart felt magnetized to him in a way she could not explain. When she saw him in person the very next day, her feelings were even stronger and more intense. Even though Unicum had a reputation of being difficult and strong-willed, that did not scare Stephanie nor dissuade her from instantaneously loving him and *knowing* his soul. Thus began their more than twenty-one-year love story and transformational journey.

They moved to Spain a year or so later to begin a new life on a picturesque agricultural estate where Stephanie is helping to develop a new concept of natural animal feed as well as working as the stable manager for transit horses. She has always been very connected to animals and nature and has a strong intuitive sense for their needs and desires, so it made sense that she gravitated to working with them. She has always been very sensitive to the energy and emotions of those around her, which made her feel overwhelmed and unsafe at times.

✳ *It is common for overly sensitive people to lean into the safety of animals.*

Stephanie describes Unicum as a highly intelligent ancient soul, a dignified warrior, and loyal protector of those he loves. For the first time in her life, she felt utterly and completely safe with another being, and she fully trusted him to protect her in ways she was never shielded as a child. Even when she isn't physically with him, she can tangibly feel their heart and soul connection.

Once while Stephanie was in the field with some young cattle that were acting a bit unruly toward her, Unicum jumped his fence and firmly planted himself between his mom and the cattle in a very protective manner. She'd never experienced a horse (or person) defending her with such fierceness, and she had mixed emotions of both loving his safeguarding and yet at the same time feeling unworthy of such devotion and loyalty from another being.

Both Stephanie and Unicum unwillingly left their families way too early in their lives and were forced to become the "strong one." Stephanie's strict education ingrained in her that being strong, versus soft and sensitive, was crucial for survival, safety, and success in a callous world, even if this meant disallowing your true nature. They'd also both known and loved others who ultimately betrayed or left them. In turn, both of these beautiful beings put armor around their hearts, and consequentially they had a plethora of unreleased anger and repressed emotional pain.

Unicum is an alpha male personality and is not a nurturing, coddling horse who puts people at ease. Stephanie observed that people do not understand him like she does, and she could relate because she often felt misunderstood and wrongly judged as being defensive and appearing unsociable, too. Stephanie and Unicum are both highly intuitive and can accurately read others. They can see into each other's soul and feel the lifetimes of pain they have both experienced. This intimate *knowing* of each other that they have, in addition to the mirroring of their ways, was part of their Divine plan to come together and heal their emotional wounds of betrayal and abandonment.

They have both deeply loved and cared for other beings; when they do, there's nothing they wouldn't do for them. Fiercely loyal, they want to take away the pain of those they love. They have repeatedly been betrayed or abandoned by those closest to them, which corroborated their internal stories that they cannot trust other beings with their hearts.

Unicum has deeply loved only a few animals on the farm, and in true Unicum style, he ardently led and protected them. Unfortunately, each of those animals developed physical issues that took their lives much sooner than expected. He was beside himself, mad with pain, upon losing his most beloved horse companion, Seabiscuit. He exhibited much sadness and depression with each loss, and he would stop eating for some time. Stephanie felt the losses as deeply as he did, especially Seabiscuit, whom they were both very emotionally connected to for many lives. Stephanie loves her animals with her whole heart and will do anything possible to prevent any of them from having any pain, and she would often blame herself, thinking she hadn't done enough to help them, which created even more pain and grief.

Through many difficult animal losses several years ago, Stephanie rediscovered her innate capacity to communicate with animals, which had been buried since childhood, along with her naturally sensitive disposition. She longed to understand more about humans' spiritual connection with animals to aid in her grieving process and honor the amazing animals that had forever changed her for the better.

Around this time, Stephanie had clearly established that her animals reflected her and realized there was more to uncover about animal *mirroring*. She'd already been sharing and utilizing what she'd learned from her animals to help others, and she decided to search for a website domain name that reflected this approach of helping animals and people heal through their mirroring for a new project. This web search is what "accidentally" led Stephanie to my books, classes, and healing services.

From the onset of their first Tandem Healing session, Stephanie declared that her intentions were to dive into the deeper emotional work with her beloved Unicum to heal their mirroring wounds. With passion and enthusiasm, Stephanie embarked on a healing journey to reveal her authentic self and learn that she is worthy and deserving of *her own* love and trust. She also wanted to integrate and heal her Divine feminine that had been denied, neglected, abused, and repressed her entire life by a strict and rigid inner masculine warrior.

Stephanie had also experienced invasiveness by an overcontrolling, cold, and unpleasable parent, which was compounded by the educational system she was placed into early in her life. Because of this, her inner child was programmed to be a people pleaser and thought that no matter how much she did for herself, her partner, or her animals, it was never enough. She'd consistently blame herself for falling short of the outcome she desired, assuming she must be inadequate, not good enough, and unlovable. It was a vicious masochistic pattern that she dearly longed to change.

With healthy internal parenting, commitment, and compassion, Stephanie was able to jump the hurdles of her heart to become more empowered from within and know that she is worthy of the same level of care and love that she has provided endless animals. It hasn't been an easy process, but she valiantly created the internal parenting needed for the deeper releases to unfold to lighten her load and free herself of the binds of her past. She is now beginning to believe more and more that she is worthy of her *own* love and that she can trust *herself* as much as she trusts Unicum.

These two brave and beautiful lightworkers submerged themselves in the shadows of their past wounds in this life, and previous ones, where they had been repeatedly betrayed and abandoned. They released an overabundance of anger, grief, and emotional pain because they were finally ready to drop their weapons and liberate themselves from lifetimes of trauma and heartache. With the removal of layer after layer of protection from their hearts, they surrendered to a higher power and created space for more love and gratitude to set up shop in their souls. I witnessed many momentous and moving occasions working with them that revealed their immense capacity to love themselves through the pain of their pasts.

Unicum & Stephanie
Photo by Yuliya Dubrovina Photography

These days Stephanie and Unicum are feeling lighter, more authentic, and compassionate. People that have known Unicum for many years (osteopath, farrier, vet, etc.) have each mentioned the positive changes in his behavior without realizing the emotional healing work that has transpired. Stephanie shared that his demeanor and energy have dramatically shifted. He is more tender, kinder, and more at peace with her and other humans. She feels he has healed his past betrayal wounds, and with her new level of awareness she also recognizes that the positive shifts she sees in him are beautifully reflecting her growth. Stephanie is now enthusiastically working in the healing arts for animals and their people via several holistic modalities, including animal communication.

---✦---

Transformational Soul Practice
Healing the Heart

Reflections: *Journal your thoughts and observations of what this story has brought into your awareness for your growth. Seek the nugget or gift for you to embrace.*

What part brought up the most emotion?
Can you see yourself or your animal in Stephanie and Unicum?
Have you repressed your sensitive attributes?
Is there protection around your heart?

Try creating a regular gratitude practice. Find three things to be grateful for daily, and then feel the gratitude in your heart and allow that feeling to expand. Gratitude is like a jackhammer to the armor around our heart.

Angels and Lifesavers
Andrea & Monty

Andrea Montgomery will *never* forget the year 2010. It's the year that her dear mother was placed in a memory care facility with Alzheimer's (she passed one year later); her brother had recently been diagnosed with the early onset of Parkinson's disease; her closest and dearest friend in the world was going through a difficult stretch of time with mental illness; and her then-husband, who was an unemployed alcoholic, was diagnosed with laryngeal cancer. Andrea had just awakened to realize she valued herself enough to envision leaving him when the cancer was detected, stopping her in her tracks.

Andrea had always taken care of the needs of others before herself, but during this challenging period of her life she was struggling and burned out. And through it all an unwavering voice in her head persistently declared that it was the perfect time to get a puppy. Even Andrea was surprised at her steadfast focus and desire to adopt a young dog, despite opposition from her then-husband. It felt as if she had a Divine appointment of utmost importance.

At four months of age, Monty was wandering the streets of a small town in rural Washington State. An angel picked him up and took him to the local humane society. On the day before he was to be euthanized, another angel from a no-kill rescue organization decided to save Monty and put him into a foster home. Once these heavenly caretakers gave him some love and tended to his medical needs, they listed him as adoptable.

Whenever there are "saving angels" involved, it is a sign that the animal has a spiritual reservation and purposeful mission ahead.

Meeting Monty was the saving grace of Andrea's difficult year. As soon as his foster mom opened up the baby gate, Monty jaunted directly over to Andrea and flopped into her lap. She swears her heart opened in that very moment and it hasn't closed since. The adorable five-month-old pup instantaneously brought joy and a level of unconditional love to Andrea that she had never felt before. In that moment she suddenly realized just how much she'd been slowly dying inside.

Monty's love not only raised her vibration, it showed her the way out of her destructive marriage. He surrounded her heart with so much love that she could finally begin to heal, grow, and allow in a healthy relationship. Andrea is now happily married to a kind, loving, and giving man who also dearly loves Monty. Monty and Andrea have always enjoyed spending hours on end in nature exploring, playing, and going on long runs. They've learned that their time together in nature is a crucial component of nourishing their souls and maintaining a higher frequency.

Given that Andrea and Monty's energy is enmeshed in a close soul-to-soul relationship, Monty is likely Andrea's best spiritual teacher. There is nothing Monty could ever do that would prevent his wonderful mom from adoring, loving, and cherishing him. Andrea stated that she has never loved another being with such unbounded and infinite love, and that when Monty transitions, he will take the best part of her with him. Now that Monty is almost eleven years of age, she often fears the dreadful day of his eventual passing, and that the pain of his loss would be too much for her bear. These types of statements are indications of an interdependent relationship. Every animal lover has likely been in Andrea's shoes before with an animal who brought them a paradigm—changing amount of light and love, yet might not realize that what they see in their animal is also within themselves. Typically, these once or twice-in-a-lifetime soul-bond relationships are animals in our soul group and we have incarnated together many times for our mutual growth.

Andrea's mother had always longed to give birth to her own children but assumed she could not conceive throughout the years of her first marriage. Then she divorced and remarried and, miraculously, got pregnant—twice! Her world revolved around her children. She was so thrilled to have them that she lavished and smothered them with love and protection, and cared for their every need and desire. Her over-loving ways proliferated, and understandably so, when Andrea was diagnosed at four years old with an atrial septal defect of the heart and a tumor on her spine. She had both open-heart and open-chest surgery simultaneously and can clearly remember fearfully looking at her mom when they wheeled her off to surgery.

As Andrea and her brother grew into adults, they felt the pressure of continuing to fulfill their mother's needs, and on some level knew they were responsible for her happiness. After she passed it was clear to them that their loving mother had a hole within that she was trying to fill with them, which unknowingly and unintentionally created codependent relationships grounded in *conditional* love.

Andrea's mother modeled for her children a more external type of love, one that needed others to fill her with love so she would feel lovable, versus unconditionally loving herself first and then empowering her children to feel independent and self-assured. This is very common for many mothers of both two-legged and four-legged children and is rooted in not getting their own needs met early in life.

When I first heard from Andrea, she had been observing her love—and fear—around her soulmate Monty from a higher perspective, and she wanted to work on keeping her heart open even during heartbreak. She also recognized the parallels of her mom's fears and needs. Monty has gifted her endless glimpses of fabulous 5D living, and because he is a such a high vibrating joy-bringer, she sought to learn how to maintain that vibration more often, regardless of external issues that might trigger her into anxiety and fear.

Monty had always exhibited traits of the Needy One profile that I share in *Soul Healing with Our Animal Companions*, which is rooted in the abandonment he experienced early in his life. In addition to being a wonderful light, he is also over-the-top vocal, and very needy, jealous, and high maintenance due to his physical and emotional issues. Andrea is very aware of just how much Monty responds to her feelings and emotions, and this motivates her to dive deeper into his teachings for her to heal deep-seated emotional wounds so he doesn't absorb or reflect them back to her.

Their extraordinary sacred soul partnership has been healing and transformational for them both. Through Monty's teachings in what he reflects for her, Andrea is learning to shift a longstanding pattern of filling others before filling herself.

This process requires releasing control and unconditionally loving ourselves and those under our care. Connecting to a higher frequency through meditation to create safety and developing healthy internal parenting grounded in self-love will bring monumental growth. This is a great place to begin.

Monty

Typically, there are deep-seated emotional wounds longing to be released that will naturally clear with your strong intention and desire to do the inner healing work.

Monty's wayshower attributes awakened Andrea to a benevolent way of *being* and to the realization that the light she sees in Monty beautifully mirrors her lovable, authentic self. More each day, she is beginning to believe that she is enough, that she is doing the best she can, and that tending to her own garden is the greatest gift she can give those she loves. Nowadays, Andrea is a conservationist and animal communicator in Washington state. She consistently strives to stay connected to the universe and lean into its nurturing support and guidance, which created everything that is near and dear to her, especially Monty.

Andrea and Monty are both courageous warriors of light, ushering in a new Earth through their conscious personal journeys and their important work in the world.

Monty and Andrea

— ✳ —

Transformational Soul Practice
Releasing Fear

Reflections: Journal your thoughts and observations of what this story has brought into your awareness for your growth. Seek the nugget or gift for you to embrace.

What part brought up the most emotion?
Can you see yourself or your animals in Andrea or Monty?
Do you have an elevated level of fear around losing your animal companion?

- *Sit for five minutes each day intentionally connecting to and allowing in love from your light team and Higher Self.*
- *Allow them to fill you with unconditional love of the highest vibration possible by breathing deeply directly into your heart, while imagining their love filling you and going to every cell in your body; visualize their love moving throughout every fiber of your being.*
- *When you feel lovable and connected to a higher level of consciousness, you'll automatically have less fear.*
- *If you catch yourself worrying about something you can't control, pull back your energy, breathe, and center yourself in the present moment.*
- *Breathe in compassion for yourself. (Hold for four seconds.)*
- *Breathe out love for all beings.*
- *Consciously tap into the stream of 5D consciousness and sense the safety and peace.*

In the depth of winter, I finally learned that within me there lay an invincible summer.

ALBERT CAMUS

8

The Enlightened Luminaries

Unconditional love really exists within each of us. It is part of our deep inner being. It is not so much an active emotion as a state of being.

RAM DASS

Sometimes there are animals that unmistakably stand out as being old souls and wayshowers. This absolutely does not make them special or better than other animals, it merely means that they've evolved to the place on their souls' journey wherein they have mastered the ability to hold and anchor more light and maintain a higher frequency. These enlightened luminaries are eager to take on the responsibility of being a wayshower and will intentionally spread joy and love onto as many beings as possible. They graciously help their person and all those they meet with such stoic ease and grace that you'd never believe they had ever known sorrow.

All those that have gone before us have learned endless lessons to reach the point of choosing to lovingly serve others. These are the masters we all want to emulate and eagerly seek to absorb their wise teachings. The older souls have a knowing of what each of us is growing into right now during this incredible time on our planet, and they are here to contribute to our shift to a higher dimension. These two-legged *and* four-legged beings are keenly aware that we will all get through the grueling 3D polarity experiences our souls have created for our growth and learn that it is safe to let go of the need to control our lives, and bathe in the unity field of consciousness that *is* love.

✳   *Let us all intentionally give ourselves permission to feel love more intimately and allow it to revolutionize our lives.*

The following stories are not only about two incredible animal wayshowers—for their humans are more than merely along for the ride with them. They are wayshowers, too, and want to make a positive difference in the world. It was no coincidence that these beautiful lightworkers were magnetized to be together, for at the centers of their sacred partnerships were higher plans and purposeful missions that revealed themselves through their love story.

As you read each story, empower it to gift you with a teaching in your highest and best.

Shamanic Joy-Bringer
Ruby & Bella

In the summer of 2009, almost a year after the loss of her beloved dog Tess, Ruby Falconer felt drawn to explore the photos of the adoptable canines on the local humane society's website. Her attention was drawn to an adorable young golden retriever mix who had one blue eye and one brown eye. Ruby is a Shamanic Egyptian Astrologer who is deeply committed to and immersed in living a shamanic lifestyle. She immediately recognized the spiritual significance of the different eye colors—the ability to see into two worlds simultaneously: the Earth world (the brown eye), and the Spirit world (the blue eye). She decided to go meet her at the next available adoption fair.

Ruby immediately loved four-month-old Bella. She was friendly, kind, and had this irresistible smile on her face. Nonetheless, it was a big decision and Ruby wanted to be certain, so she sat in her car and watched Bella interact with the other dogs. She observed that Bella wasn't a barker and, in true Pisces form, she was easygoing and friendly to all beings. Still waffling, Ruby suddenly, unmistakably, heard the spirit of Tess, her dog that had transitioned the previous year, say "Adopt her. NOW!" Ruby reacted immediately and went inside and began filling out paperwork just in the nick of time. Another couple arrived moments later in the hope of adopting her, too. Tess had intervened to ensure that the two shamans were brought together!

Right from the beginning, Bella was an absolute delight and loved everyone she met. This included all humans, dogs, cats, and even Ruby's green-winged macaw. Ruby lives in an intentional spiritual community filled with animal lovers, and there are often visitors on the property taking a course or workshop at their retreat center. One thing was certain: everyone felt lighter after connecting with Bella, and that included every animal in the community—even the dogs that didn't get along with other dogs. Everyone adored Bella's infectious loving nature and looked forward to experiencing the joy, acceptance, and unconditional love that she effortlessly showered on each of them. It was as if her mission was to remind each and every being that they are sparks of the Divine, and to know that they mattered and are so very lovable.

Bella became the much-loved matriarch dog of the neighborhood, but her heart endearingly belonged to her mom. Ruby and Bella were inseparable. Never had Ruby felt more loved in her entire life. Be it the next room or the grocery store, wherever her mom was going is where Bella wanted to be. When Ruby was doing her inner-soul work or working with clients, Bella was always close by, holding Transformational Healing Presence.

Many times during Bella's life, Ruby experienced perceived betrayals and disappointments. Like a ray of unavoidable sunshine, Bella would eagerly remind her of the beauty and wonder in life and within all beings. Bella was relentlessly positive and always taught that community and being with others was important for our soul growth. She was always happiest upon seeing another person or animal, and in turn, she raised the vibration of the collective consciousness. Plain and simple, she loved serving others and made a point of always modeling that behavior for everyone.

Ruby shared a story of when a stray, emaciated, pregnant Plott hound showed up on their property and the entire community rallied around the situation to assist the fear-filled canine. Mollie Mae was given food but would only eat when humans weren't around. Soon, she had her puppies under one of the cabins, all twelve of them, though one was stillborn. Adamant about helping the pups get socialized and cared for, Ruby and others were able to relocate the eleven puppies into Ruby's small fenced-in yard, in a tentlike shelter with tarps and blankets. Thankfully, Mollie Mae began feeding her pups in the new area, even though she still highly distrusted humans. The high fence could not contain Mollie Mae however, and she consistently jumped it to get away from the pups after doing the bare minimum mothering role of feeding and cleaning them.

Bella was immediately curious about the pups and wanted to be involved in their care. It was no surprise that Mollie Mae instantly trusted and was drawn to dear Bella too. They became best friends. Bella grounded her and helped her to understand more of the ways of humans. In response to Mollie Mae's detached mothering style, Bella stepped up and lovingly embraced the role of surrogate mom to the puppies. Bella oversaw all puppy interactions with the neighbors that arrived daily to help socialize them. One night, Bella and Mollie Mae sounded the alarm that a bobcat was outside, and after that the puppies were always brought indoors after dusk. Without missing a beat, Bella nurtured and guided the pups to help them to adjust to the changes in their routine. They cherished their "second mom."

All eleven puppies were adopted into wonderful homes, and Mollie Mae spent six additional months in "Bella and Ruby School" learning that humans can be trustworthy and loving, and that it was safe to open her heart. Soon thereafter, she was adopted by a caring and compassionate family that loves her very much. It's easy to see how vital and instrumental Bella's role was in the care of the puppies and of Mollie Mae. She was a pivotal early influencer for their emotional development and evolution. These are actions of a wayshower.

At eleven years of age, Bella developed physical ailments that ultimately she could not recover from. Ruby held sacred space and tried hard to create an option for Bella to heal and stay, should that be the path she chose, but it was her time. We worked together in her final weeks, and I could see Bella's Higher Self ready to welcome her home on the other side. She was a blessing to hundreds of people and animals over the course of her joy-filled meaningful life. When Bella transitioned on Earth Day,

Bella

Bella, Mollie Mae, and pups

April 22, 2020, the entire community mourned the loss of this luminous soul. She made an extraordinarily positive difference for others during her time on Earth. Bella regularly visits Ruby during her meditations and soul journeys, and she senses that Bella is patiently awaiting the day that they will be lovingly reunited.

Bella teaches us that we, too, can live in two worlds simultaneously and feel the expansiveness of Divine love such that it effortlessly flows from our hearts to all beings.

Transformational Soul Practice
Connecting to your Higher Self

Reflections: *Journal your thoughts and observations of what this story has brought into your awareness for your growth. Seek the nugget or gift for you to embrace.*

What part brought up the most emotion?
Can you see yourself or your animal in Ruby and Bella?
Journal any insights or thoughts that reading Bella's story has brought into your awareness.

Now is the perfect time for you to send gratitude to any animal that popped into your mind (and heart) when you read about Bella's life as a wayshower. Expressing gratitude will open you to a new level of healing, which automatically lays out the welcome mat to allow in more love.

Bella was a master of staying connected to the frequency of joy and love. It feels as if she was deeply connected to her Higher Self and Divine Love in each and every moment. Creating a habit to commune more intimately with your Higher Self is a powerful way to begin living more like Bella did.

Here's an effective and beneficial exercise to aid in your conscious connection to your Divine Higher Self:

1. *Sit quietly and focus on your breath.*
2. *Let your thoughts go by, bringing your attention to your heart.*
3. *Consciously ask to connect to your Divine Higher Self.*
4. *Remain open and receptive as you sink into this sacred connection and commune with the all-knowing part of yourself.*
5. *Express gratitude to your Divine Higher Self and the beings of light that serve your growth, both two-legged and four-legged.*

Using this exercise daily has the ability to aid in your spiritual growth and enhance your levels of abundance, love, empowerment, and wisdom.

The Noble One
Elaine & Maverick

They called Maverick's birth an "accident." A quarter horse stud jumped his fence and beelined to the cute palomino Tennessee Walker mare and, well, what came out of that union was anything but an accident. Unfortunately for the farmer, he simply could not foresee any potential with the young horse. He never rode him and for the most part left him by himself in a separate field. After a year or two he decided he would sell the horse, and if he couldn't, he intended to take him to auction.

Elaine's birth was also unplanned. Her parents weren't intending a second baby anytime soon. Her one-year-old brother's high needs demanded most of her mother's attention. Much like Maverick, Elaine was the quiet one, more or less off in the background. The good news is that there wasn't anything unplanned about Elaine and Maverick's impending journey together.

Elaine's childhood was filled with one painful experience after the next. Her parents divorced when she was two and both quickly moved on to new relationships. Her father's long-time girlfriend, whom she loved and had grown awfully close to, passed from cancer when Elaine was nine years old. She unfortunately never had a close relationship with her birth mother and always felt like she was an inconvenience. Even worse, Elaine was repeatedly sexually molested by someone she should have been able to trust.

Through it all there was one saving grace: horses. From the moment Elaine could express herself, everyone around her knew that she was obsessed with horses. Every birthday, Christmas, and any other potential occasion in which a gift might be forthcoming, her parents knew that a horse was at the top of their daughter's wish list. Right before Elaine's thirteenth birthday, her father heard tale of a man wanting to sell his unbroke horse for a good price, and off they went to check him out.

They walked into the pasture where the murky-looking small horse was located, and it immediately responded to them. He walked directly to Elaine, sniffed her jacket, and then his eyes lit up and sparkled as if he suddenly recognized the person he'd been waiting for! Like a peacock that was performing a mating dance showing off his beautiful plumes, Maverick joyfully began prancing around them in circles, celebrating the reunion of their souls. Then he abruptly returned to Elaine and began gently sniffing her face, and sealed the deal by giving her a big slurpy kiss on her cheek.

In the year or two prior to meeting Maverick, Elaine had been sneaking out of the house to hang out with shady friends and

Maverick and Elaine in their early years together
Photo by Kelly Lynn Photography

getting into fights at school. This rebellious behavior was fueled by her previous emotional wounds and trauma. Underneath it all she felt hopeless and didn't care much about herself or her life. All of this changed the moment Maverick walked up to her on that day and said: I see you. You matter. You are lovable. And Elaine felt exactly the same way about him.

It wasn't an option to pay someone to saddle break him, so her father declared that it was up to Elaine. By that point in her life, she'd had many riding lessons and had avidly read just about every horse-related book that was in print. She was confident she could navigate her way through it.

A few weeks later, her father dropped her off at the barn with a raggedy halter, a lead rope, and some brushes. Miraculously, by the time her dad returned to pick her up hours later, Elaine was riding Maverick bareback with such beauty and grace it was as if they'd been riding together forever. He never once spooked or tried to buck. With the patience of an old soul, he calmly allowed an incredible and beautiful bonding moment to naturally unfold.

Maverick was the compassionate, caring, grounding, and consistent bright light that Elaine had always longed for in her life. She had a bottomless pit of pent-up anger back then, and sometimes she'd redirect it onto Maverick. In those moments he stood very still and calm, as if he were holding sacred space and had made a conscious choice to create a safe place for Elaine to release her pain. Over time, his unconditional love allowed her to begin removing the barriers around her heart. Maverick paved the way for Elaine to feel hopeful about life again by demonstrating the wayshower virtues of kindness, courage, and integrity with utmost perfection.

Elaine wasn't the only one who was forever changed by Maverick. On one occasion while she and Maverick were showing at the county fair, Elaine was talking to Lily, the younger sister of a girlfriend who'd previously been bucked off of a horse. Lily's traumatic experience had resulted in a broken arm and a concussion, and she'd been terrified of horses ever since. Elaine asked Lily to hold Maverick's lead line so she could quickly run to the restroom. With much reassurance of Maverick's gentle ways from Elaine, she ultimately agreed. Upon returning, Elaine found Lily giggling while Maverick nuzzled her hair. With the brilliance of a master healer Maverick had helped her to reconcile her previous traumatic experience. Days later Lily was fearlessly riding Maverick! Lily and her sister eventually went on to open a therapeutic horse riding facility for children with all types of challenges—emotional, physical, and mental—where they could also be healed through the wisdom, nobility, and healing energy of horses.

Hundreds of children have been on Maverick's back during

his twenty-two years. Elaine has always moved Maverick with her wherever her journey took her, even to college. The stable managers where he was boarded always knew that Maverick loved introducing children to the healing ways of horses. He was renowned as the calm, dependable horse that could be trusted with your child's life, even if they had disabilities. Many times, parents would put their child on his back and just let him walk away without holding the lead, knowing that this old soul was worthy of their respect and would predictably take them for a calm walk and return them to their parent. He was also frequently the main attraction at a child's birthday party, and he loved every moment of it.

Maverick is an extraordinary wayshower, here to teach kindness and compassion to endless people, especially during the more formidable periods of their lives.

During her college years, Elaine started shifting old patterns and going within to reflect more. She began regularly attending a yoga class, which not only organically tended to her energy field but also the connection and peace derived from the poses significantly helped her to begin controlling her thoughts and calm her anger.

There was also a moment that she will never forget that resulted from unexpectedly having to walk 1.5 miles to campus in -23 degree weather. The entire walk she was seething with anger and feeling victimized, until she reached campus and was suddenly stopped in her tracks by God's handiwork. In front of her was the most glorious sunrise she'd ever seen. The rays of sunshine were magically glistening on the fresh pure snow, and Elaine felt the purity of the magnificent vision throughout every fiber of her being. In that sacred, unforgettable spiritual moment, Elaine had an epiphany and said to herself, *I almost missed this because I was so angry.* From that day forward, she made a conscious decision to look at all beings with compassionate eyes and was committed to seeking out the beauty that is always there in the world.

Elaine then became aware of her guilt and remorse for any pain she might have inflicted upon her beloved horse companion when she was younger. The next time she saw Maverick, through a bucketful of tears, she sought his forgiveness for the times she'd unknowingly redirected her pain and anger onto him. Without missing a beat, in true Maverick style, he moved in closer to her and emitted deep and profound love to his most treasured and beloved student to let her know that there was nothing to forgive but herself.

Maverick and Elaine in 2021

Nowadays Elaine lives on a farm in Oklahoma with her boyfriend, six rescue horses, and, of course, Maverick. Even at twenty-two years of age, he is the well-respected lead horse that all of the other horses instinctively follow. He keeps order in the barn through gentle, peaceful ways. A year or two ago Elaine began learning more about the spiritual healing abilities of horses while asking a question about one of her horses on Mustang Maddy's social media group, and someone suggested that she read my first book to learn more about healing with our animals and how they mirror us.

You see, Maverick has always reflected the noble, wise sage part of Elaine that was unknowingly repressed and kept under lock and key due to her unresolved childhood emotional wounds. Maverick has always had the ability to see, through the

Maverick giving pony rides at a wedding

window of Elaine's pain, her enormous capacity to love and be a beacon of light for others. More and more, Elaine is revealing her golden light to be a compass for others, and some of this is through rescuing and healing horses with a difficult past. In addition to her love of horses, Elaine is also a landscape architect specializing in native habitat restoration and creating sustainable environments for people, communities, plants, and animals. Her passion is mitigating the disastrous effects that humans have on the environment, and what a beautiful way to serve our beloved planet and all of its inhabitants!

These days when she goes out to the pasture to see Maverick, his demeanor is different. He knows she is on the right path now, and they have evolved into a deep soul-to-soul friendship fueled by unconditional love. Her heart still fills with warmth and love each and every time she sees him.

---❋---

Transformational Soul Practice
Invoking Self-Forgiveness

Reflections: Journal your thoughts and observations of what their story has brought into your awareness for your growth. Seek the nugget or gift for you to embrace.

What part brought up the most emotion?
Can you see yourself or your animal in Elaine or Maverick?

Elaine mentioned that one of Maverick's most powerful gifts was teaching her about forgiveness. Self-forgiveness is the key to bridging the gap to self-love, which is the cure to most things you want to change in your life. Once you forgive yourself for any perceived bad choices, you are then free to love yourself, receive love from others, and allow in more loving experiences. In honor of Maverick's beautiful teachings and Elaine's courageous journey:

1. Sit in quiet reflection and bring your focus to your heart. Take several deep breaths.
2. Call in the beings of light who work with you to support you. Lean into their love.
3. Ask your heart to show you a particular incident that needs your forgiveness. It might be something you are judging or feeling guilty about.
4. Acknowledge the incident and activate it in your psyche.
5. Sense where you are holding this pain in your body and how it has shown up in your life.
6. Breathe love and light into that area of your body and allow the gentle release of the self-inflicted pain.
7. Accept the fact that you cannot change the past, and that you did the best you knew how to do at the time.
8. Close your eyes, put your hands on your heart, and say to yourself: I know you did the best you could. I forgive you and I love you. (Repeat until you feel it.)
9. Thank yourself for having the courage and desire to shift this pattern of being hard on yourself.
10. Make an intention to be kinder and more compassionate to yourself.
11. Express gratitude to your spirit guides, angels, animals, and beings of light for their support.

You can repeat this exercise whenever you notice you are thinking about a past event with remorse or guilt and are ready to receive the next level of self-forgiveness to raise your vibration.

9

Sacred Service of the Heart

In loving one another through our works we bring an increase of grace and a growth in divine love.

MOTHER TERESA

Most seekers who are walking a spiritual path believe that some form of sacred service is essential to our spiritual growth and evolution. Sacred service, however large or small, opens us to reveal the highest, most Divine aspect of ourselves. Plain and simple, helping others helps us. How you serve other beings and our beautiful planet is uniquely individual, and each form or type of work becomes a sacred service to others through infusing it with love. The more you love what you do, the more substantial your contribution is to raising the vibration of the collective consciousness.

I believe this is why many millennials are unwilling to compromise their desire to find rewarding work that they love. We are waking up to the guidance of our hearts and following our own unique paths. As humanity cooperatively is moving toward a 5D frequency, we realize the importance of maintaining a higher vibration, and one of the ways to do that is through our work. As more and more people awaken to their sacred roles, we move closer than ever before to creating heaven on Earth.

Consciously joining forces with your animals to serve others will create unimaginable beauty on our Earth. Many animals and their humans have deliberately chosen to participate in this significant transitional period and are guiding our planet to 5D living through tending to their own vibrations and helping others to do the same. Our animal kin serve to remind us of our connection to the Universe and have the innate ability to hold space for us to wake up to our sacred tasks.

In this chapter, you will read about three remarkable light warrior teams making powerful impacts in our world through their contributions to raising the frequency of our planet through ways large and small. Reading about their inspirational lives most assuredly will open your heart. You might even recognize a part of yourself in their actions. Sometimes we are unaware of how we (and our animals) are already showing up for others as guiding lights, so be sure to breathe in love and gratitude for yourself upon noticing your reflection in their actions.

As I mentioned in chapter 1, it is possible that one of your spirit guides or peers in your soul group (or extended soul group) will incarnate into the physical temple of one of your animals to team up with you to serve more beings, or to help support you in profound and meaningful ways that you will probably never forget. Whatever the reason, you will feel so intensely connected with the animal that it will be life and heart altering for your evolutionary journey. Many of the example stories in this book have made me wonder if indeed this type of soul incarnation is (or was) the case with an animal, but none more than the ones written about in this chapter.

As you read each story, empower it to gift you with a teaching in your highest and best.

Compassionate Master Healers
Maura & Blue

Maura Finn moved to Guatemala in 2009 for a position as an English coordinator and teacher at a bilingual ecological school. It was a wonderful position, and she found it extremely rewarding because the school was sustainably driven and focused just as much on the youths' social and emotional growth as it did on their mental development. Maura was fully absorbed with her gratifying work at the school and was making a positive difference for the students *and* the teachers.

While she'd always loved animals, Maura had never fully recovered from the loss of her childhood soulmate dog, Chips, who'd transitioned when she was nine years old. At that time, she was inconsolable and cried daily for many, many years, mourning his loss. Adopting a dog while living in Guatemala was never part of her plan. She was uncertain how long she'd be in the country, and it simply didn't make sense to get attached to an animal at that point in her life.

The first time she met Blue he affectionately jumped up on his hind legs and put his paws on her shoulders and smiled. Maura instantly felt a deep love and warm connection with him as she laughed and looked into his soulful eyes. Her laughter was mainly prompted by the fact that they were the exact same height!

She was only supposed to dog-sit the beautiful three-year-old canine for a couple of weeks while her friend went to Europe to visit his ailing father. He had rescued the unsocialized canine a few months prior from a man who'd unfortunately kept him in a cage all the time and was planning to euthanize him. As fate would have it, Maura's friend needed to stay in Europe much longer than anticipated and gave her the option of moving Blue to another home he'd lined up, or she could keep Blue for herself. After their three weeks of blissful time together, Maura knew without an inkling of doubt that it was their destiny to be together.

Blue blossomed under Maura's patient and loving ways. After a period of time helping him with his socialization skills, Blue felt completely comfortable and safe interacting with other dogs and humans. Maura and Blue would clock endless hours hiking through the forest and mountains just outside of the city. Because they were always walking somewhere together, and because they both embodied joy and had loving, accepting demeanors, they were soon well known and beloved by many townsfolk.

Blue

Everywhere they walked, people driving by would yell "Blue!" Children in the central park ran to greet Blue and even though they didn't know how to speak English, they knew "Blue" because of how generously he shared his love with each of them. Even babies would light up and squeal with joy upon seeing the lightworker pooch and his kind mom.

During their walks, strangers would initially be drawn to stop and pet Blue, but this often transitioned into the person disclosing to Maura something that was heavy on their heart. Her innate healing abilities and schooling had prepared her to naturally ease the pain of others. Blue would identify who needed healing, and together they would provide a loving space for healing to transpire. People were magnetized to the duo, instinctively trusting that it was safe for them to share something intimate.

After five years in Guatemala, Maura felt drawn to return to the States, and of course she wasn't going anywhere without Blue! She felt called to delve into a deeper inner transformational journey that was beckoning her so loudly she could no longer ignore it. Maura had observed that it was common for Blue to take on her emotional and physical ailments, which further motivated her to take the plunge into a new level of shadow work.

She intuitively knew that it was necessary work that would pave the way for her to hold a higher frequency and serve more beings. During that emotional period of time, Blue amped up his support and helped to heal her childhood trauma. He was Maura's inner child's emotional support companion, and he would lay at her feet during intense healing sessions with practitioners, then comfort and console her afterward. His grounded, compassionate love never wavered as Maura took a courageous deep dive into the crevasses of her pain. Blue showed her the way back to her heart and helped her to reveal a new level of empowerment and peace.

Maura accepted a position as a crisis support specialist in a rural high school in North Carolina. Often Blue would accompany her at the school to provide his special brand of therapeutic services to the students. This dynamic healing duo would sometimes tour the students' classrooms together. Blue would walk up and down the aisles as each of the teens petted him, all the while profoundly shifting the mood in the room with his compassionate ways. Sometimes he would stop at the desk of one particular student that he instinctively knew needed him most. On one occasion, the "chosen" student followed them into the hall with tears in his eyes and disclosed how much Blue's affection meant to him. Apparently two days prior his dog had passed away, and he'd been having a difficult time.

Students often arrived in Maura's office with anger, anxiety, or panic attacks. Then they'd see Blue and would run their fingers through his golden hair, and suddenly they were regulated enough for Maura to proceed with the deeper inner healing work. One of Maura's past students reached out to her recently to convey that, to this day, Blue is still guiding him on his journey. Apparently Blue shows up in his dreams to bring the youth clarity when making big decisions. Several of Maura's clients over the years have also revealed that Blue has provided consolation to them in their dreams, so being a dream traveler is another of the ways in which he serves.

Blue and Maura's sacred healing partnership never wavered and their reach was substantial. Maura has held various positions grounded in helping youth and adults heal from trauma, all the while growing her private healing practice utilizing several energy, psychology, and spiritual healing modalities. Maura and Blue's healing endeavors always had a beautiful synchronistic flow to them, as if their souls were intrinsically and intentionally connected on behalf of creating something bigger than them both.

Undoubtedly, Blue and Maura are connected through their soul group, or spiritual family, and have been together in many lifetimes. As I shared in chapter 4, our spiritual families are composed of beings sharing a similar frequency, that we repeatedly collaborate with to grow and evolve, and we predictably have an intensely strong bond. The first time Maura visited her childhood home with Blue, she discovered that he is indeed her childhood dog, Chips! Nothing brought her more happiness than knowing that she was blessed to be with the same amazing soul again.

I was blessed to meet Maura at a book signing in Sylva, North Carolina, and had the honor of working with Blue to prepare his transition back to spirit. In his last week or two Maura would frequently lie on the floor with him and talk about their life together. During these sometimes very emotional and revered moments together, Maura would express through her pain that she longed to go with him, for she couldn't imagine life without her soul partner. One evening Blue spoke to her telepathically and said: *You have so much to do here. This was our contract. If you only knew how much more I could help you from the other side.* Then he showed her images of all the places she would soon visit, which included England, India, and an island in Thailand.

After Blue's sacred transition back to spirit, Maura purchased a one-way ticket to Scotland on faith. Her journeys have taken her to England, India, and then Thailand, and she currently resides on the exact island Blue showed her on that unforgettable evening. Maura now has a thriving healing practice in Thailand administering to both humans and animals. Blue's ashes are spread all over the world, and the best part is that his spirit has continued to guide and support Maura on every step of her journey. Their mutual devotion and sacred work continues, just in a different way. They communicate each month through *Letters from Blue,* which are essentially Divine Love Letters to assist Maura on her path that she channels from Blue's Higher Self.

Blue and Maura are extraordinary examples of wayshowers anchoring a high frequency of light on Earth. Both are profoundly contributing to raising the planetary consciousness to a fifth-dimensional frequency through their purposeful work together. Blue's love is forever in the heart of every compassionate act Maura carries out on behalf of another being.

Maura and Blue

———— ✳ ————

Transformational Soul Practice
Creating Good Karma

Reflections: Journal your thoughts and observations of what this story has brought into your awareness for your growth. Seek the nugget or gift in their story for you to embrace.

What part brought up the most emotion?
Can you see yourself or your animals in Maura and Blue?

Maura and Blue beautifully represent how to be in compassionate service to all those we come into contact with. They are rock stars when it comes to performing random acts of kindness and creating positive karma.

Intentionally step into an enhanced level of kindness and compassion for all beings, including yourself. The creation of good karma can be through large or small acts that might bring about an overdue smile or dramatically shift a person's life in a positive direction. All pure acts and good deeds bring meaning to our lives and dramatically raise our frequency. The important thing to remember is that when you gift your time, love, or prosperity, you are automatically more connected and protected by Divine forces, and this creates a continuous flow for more of the same to automatically return to you. Always give from the goodness of your heart without expecting anything in return. Here are a few foundational ideas that are at the heart of creating good karma:

- *Listen compassionately to someone with your full attention.*
- *Create a judgment-free environment in your heart.*
- *Practice radical acceptance of all beings.*
- *Be kind and compassionate to yourself.*

Healing Sound Maestros
Felicity & Bear

Felicity was on the fence about whether or not she was emotionally ready to adopt another dog. It had only been a few months since her beloved canine companions Roxie and Roscoe had transitioned, and she was still mourning their loss. Nevertheless, a little voice in heart whispered that she should go meet a five-year-old longhaired chihuahua named Bear whom a man was looking to rehome. Apparently, he and his wife had recently gone their separate ways, and since he worked as a trucker the cute canine was left home alone quite a bit.

On the way there, Felicity asked spirit for a clear sign of lovingly being chosen by the dog so it would be an easy decision. Felicity went inside the home to meet Bear, while her sister, who had come with her for moral support, talked with the man outside. As soon as she sat down on the sofa, Bear enthusiastically came running from the other side of the house and jumped up on her lap as if he were reuniting with an old friend. Then he stood up on his hind legs, placed a paw on each of her shoulders, and warmly tucked his head under her chin, as if he was saying, *You're here! You're here! Thank God you're finally here!* Feeling this undeniable loving confirmation of being chosen by Bear was all it took for Felicity's heart to begin fluttering and tears of joy to flow from her eyes. She instantaneously knew with utmost certainty that they were meant to be together.

While driving home Felicity suddenly realized just how predestined it had been for them to magically meet on that day. She began connecting the dots that originated when her sister sent her flowers to ease her pain from losing Roxie and Roscoe. The beautiful bouquet had a teddy bear in the center of it. Weeks later, in a social media group, an artist was giving away paintings of animals, and Felicity signed up to receive one. It wasn't until it arrived in the mail that she learned it was a painting of a bear. And in just the previous week she had been greeted by a black lab named Bear while looking at a new home to potentially rent. She was certain Roxie and Roscoe were behind the orchestrating of these soul whispers and had Divinely arranged their meeting so she would know love again.

The first thing Felicity did once they arrived home was open the back door to show Bear the yard. She was surprised that he sprinted off as if on a mission and ran directly to Roxie and Roscoe's burial site. Felicity gasped and held her breath as she watched him sniffing and then sitting on their gravesite. It felt as if he was honoring them and paying his respects, thanking and reassuring them as if saying, *All is well. I've got it from here, guys.* There was a deliberate and sacred feeling to his actions. Then after a bit, as if he'd accomplished what he set out to do, he suddenly ran like lightning straight back to Felicity's arms.

From their first day together Bear behaved as if all was finally right in his world, and the twosome quickly became inseparable. Felicity had shared her life with many dogs over the years, but there was something distinctly different about her soul connection with Bear. It felt so familiar and safe, as if they'd known and loved each other forever. Just seeing him would cause her heart to overflow with love. He felt like an old soul, always very grounded and confident in his demeanor. Felicity soon realized that Bear had a purposeful mission to serve others and to minister to as many people as possible.

Through their years together they moved frequently and

lived in several basement apartments that had access to the main part of the home. In each and every place, Bear's routine would undoubtedly be the same. Just before Felicity left for work each morning, he would run upstairs to spend the day with the owner of the home, and exactly at 4 p.m. he'd head downstairs to wait for her return shortly thereafter. Unfailingly upon moving out, the homeowners would share that Bear had supported them through a physically or emotionally challenging time that Felicity had been completely unaware of.

When they weren't in the house or car, Bear was often comfortably carried in a sling held safely on the front of Felicity's torso, and, naturally, wherever they went people were drawn to him like a magnet. When they were out in public, Bear would turn on like a light switch when someone stopped to greet him, always ready to bring a dose of high vibrating sunshine to their day. Over the years Felicity observed that Bear behaved one distinct way (friendly and engaging) when he was "working" and serving others, and yet, when it was just the two of them, he was frequently detached, independent, and resting. You see, Bear beautifully modeled the importance of a wayshower unapologetically taking the time they need to rest, cleanse, and renew. Bear never wanted to play or be frivolous; it seemed his entire focus in this incarnation was to help others heal and raise their vibration.

Not long after Felicity began sharing her life with Bear, she was attracted to the amazing benefits of sacred sound using Tibetan and crystal bowls, flutes, harps, and tuning forks. She immersed herself in learning more about the trade under the wing of renowned sound shaman Don Simmons. For several years she served on the Sacred Sound Ministry at her spiritual community (Unity North Atlanta), and most of the time Bear served alongside her! They would frequently represent the sound ministry during the community's weekly services and events. It was around this time that Felicity began to know and feel in her heart and soul that Bear wasn't the only healer in the house.

Bear loved it when Felicity would use her tuning forks to help him clear his energy. He would indicate which fork (frequency) he needed by leaning into it and rolling onto his back. Felicity is a highly sensitive introvert and the idea of being seen or speaking in front of others typically brought about much anxiety and stress. Then Bear came into her life and granted her the grounded confidence and safety she needed to come out of her shell. He made it easier for her to transition into serving at a greater capacity because people would indubitably focus on Bear.

Today Felicity is an intuitive sacred sound practitioner in the North Georgia mountains. She and Bear began regularly facilitating Sacred Sound Immersions in many healing centers. While Felicity would prepare the room and set up her instruments and bowls, Bear would greet attendees as they arrived and begin smoothing out their energy. Exactly five minutes before Felicity began the sound immersion, Bear would intuitively lie down in the center of the circle and begin holding sacred space. When the attendees began coming out of meditation, Bear would walk around the room and touch each and every person, as if he were anointing them and shepherding them back to this world. Then, predictably, he would single out one individual he sensed needed additional healing and lay on top of his or her torso for a few minutes.

After class, the chosen person would inevitably share with Felicity the reason he or she had been selected to receive Bear's extra love and healing, and how much better he or she felt. One young lady disclosed that she'd been in a dark depression, and during Bear's healing she felt a burst of energy release from her heart; others mentioned that they'd recently lost an animal or were going through a challenging time. Felicity never questioned Bear's ability to accurately read a room and instinctively identify which person needed an extra heaping dose of his special version of healing.

Bear made a radically positive difference for endless people, but mostly for his beloved mom. During their seven years together, Felicity completely transformed her confidence level and healing abilities, thanks to Bear showing her the way to serve others through rewarding work that she loved. I first met Felicity when she attended a workshop I facilitated, and it turned out that we were both involved with the same spiritual community. So, I am one of the blessed ones that had the honor of being on the receiving end of a heaping dose of Bear love many times over. Bear was a delight to everyone in the animal-loving congregation, and when he passed, hundreds upon hundreds mourned his loss.

This extraordinary dog embodied 5D living and a purposeful life of sacred service. It is clear that Bear and Felicity have partnered together in many lifetimes. Bear was a difficult loss for Felicity to recover from, but she will forever be grateful for his teachings and guidance to step into her power to serve others. Even though Bear received his angel wings in 2019, Felicity still senses him with her during each group she facilitates . . . working the room in the way that only he could.

Bear and Felicity

Bear healing an attendee

Bear holding sacred space

---- ✳ ----

Transformational Soul Practice
Replenishing Self-Care

Reflections: *Journal your thoughts and observations of what this story has brought into your awareness for your growth. Seek the nugget or gift for you to embrace.*

What part brought up the most emotion?
Can you see yourself or your animal in Felicity and Bear?

One of Bear's many teachings was his devotion to maintaining his vibration by adhering to his physical and spiritual needs, and consistently taking the necessary soul nourishing time to clear and replenish his energy. It is an emotionally mature, 5D decision to give yourself permission to take the time you need to rest and refuel.

Be a 5D trendsetter! Practice putting in place good self-care boundaries and allow your energy to be replenished through intentional down time. Then you will more often be grounded in the present moment to focus on whatever you are working on, be it gardening, your relationships, or your sacred work.

The Miracle Wolfs
Star Wolf & Vision Wolf

There was magic and miracles in both of their births. Linda Star Wolf's mother almost died while giving her only child life in a tumultuous birth that included a twenty-mile drive, a negative reaction to medication, and forceps held in the hands of a doctor who had been drinking. During that time in Kentucky, midwifery had been outlawed and women were forbidden to deliver babies. The nurse had no choice but to give her mother an overabundance of medication in an attempt to slow down the contractions and pause the birthing process while they waited on the male doctor to arrive. Linda's mother went unconscious with her infant stuck in the birth canal. At one point they feared she was unrecoverable, but somehow they both miraculously made it through.

As a little girl Linda was frequently described as sensitive and imaginative. She spent 75 percent of her time with her much-loved grandmother with whom she shared a mutual love of being one with the natural Earth. Her grandmother would often say that children, animals, and adults gravitated to young Linda because she was so full of light that she could "charm the bees out of the trees."

The synchronicities of Vision's entire birth event were magical from start to finish. Haggard and hungry, a pregnant stray dog was taken in by Salle Redfield and her husband James, world renowned author of *The Celestine Prophecy*. Belle, the stray dog, gave birth to seven male puppies. The first three were, unfortunately, stillborn. When the fourth pup, the so-called heart chakra* puppy, was also not breathing, Salle frantically called breathwork facilitator Linda Star Wolf who immediately sent distance energy healing to him and, miraculously, the pup began breathing.

It was as if the puppy's soul recognized Star Wolf's energy and was reminded of his soul mission and higher purpose. The first three puppies decided to remain on the other side, but after Vision came to life through Star Wolf ministering to him, he bridged the way from shadow to light and brought forth the necessary life force for the following three pups to breathe into their earthly temples.

---

*The heart chakra is the fourth of the seven chakras.

At the time, Salle mentioned to Star Wolf that perhaps the fourth puppy was hers, but she simply chuckled and gently declined. She had many travels on her schedule and an active therapy practice in Chattanooga. Frankly, she couldn't imagine creating the time needed to dedicate to a puppy. Weeks later, the Redfields invited Star Wolf and her boyfriend to visit for a few days to celebrate the New Year. After they arrived, Salle was eager for her to meet Belle and the six-week-old puppies, especially since Star Wolf had been such an integral part of their birth.

Vision took his sweet time coming out of the canine family igloo in the garage, but once he did, he walked directly over to Star Wolf and, as if he were staking a claim, intentionally plopped down directly on top of her foot. Immediately Star Wolf noticed how different his appearance was than his brothers and his birth mom. He was all white with long hair like a white wolf pup, while the others were multicolored and had short hair. That evening she began reflecting upon the many signs and synchronicities of the adorable puppy's life and how it had magically entwined with hers.

On New Year's Day 1996, Star Wolf woke up and could feel the puppy in her heart and soul and knew, beyond a shadow of a doubt, that they were meant to be together. She enthusiastically shared the news with the Redfields that she intended to begin the new year with the puppy, and they were thrilled. What she didn't realize then is how her life was about to go through a dramatic and transformational shift, and how her "vision" for the future was about to change.

When she left the Redfields' home, Star Wolf was certain his name was to be Magic due to all of the magical events that brought them together . . . until she discovered that he was a dream traveler. They'd only been on their journey for a few days when the young pup came to Star Wolf in a dream and communicated that *Magic was a very nice name, but his name is Vision.* She immediately knew that she must honor his request. Throughout their relationship, Vision frequently visited Star Wolf in her dreams.

It was evident from their very first day together that there was something uniquely different about Vision. Everywhere they went, people were captivated and over-the-top magnetized to the adorable pooch. It was as if his light was so bright that people were unconsciously drawn to it.

While waiting to board their first plane flight together, Star Wolf had him out of his crate in the airport and was approached by a Norwegian man who said, "That's a beautiful wolf." Star Wolf gently corrected him and shared that Vision was not a wolf because his mom was a beagle mix. The man continued with certainty, "Yes, he is. I raise wolves. How much would you sell him for?" When she made it clear that Vision wasn't for sale the man got more persistent and aggressive in his behavior until finally in his frustration he said, "Name your price." This would be the first of many offers from strangers that wanted to purchase Vision over the course of his lifetime.

When Vision was twelve weeks old, Star Wolf was preparing to co-facilitate a weeklong training group, and she was having difficulty securing a dog-sitter. Ultimately, she made the last-minute decision to bring him with her, though she was concerned with how the young pup would conduct himself with the group. He stole the show, of course, and everyone fell in love with him! What was truly fascinating, though, was how he instinctively tapped into the consciousness of the

Vision Wolf Pup

group. Vision intuitively knew when to lie down, remain still, and hold sacred space, as if he were energetically contributing to the higher purpose of the group. Even at that young age, and throughout his life, he never once interfered with the class by barking or being rowdy. This was the first of hundreds of training classes and breathwork groups across the nation that Vision co-facilitated with Star Wolf.

During the breathwork groups that Star Wolf facilitated, Vision would regularly circle the people lying on the ground and then suddenly pause next to someone he sensed needed extra support. Instinctively following his internal guidance, he'd lick that person's foot, or place a paw on their heart, or maybe lie down beside them. The responses from the people would vary depending on what he helped them tap into and how they release energy. Some attendees would burst into tears or suddenly explode with laughter. Often times, they'd lovingly embrace him with heartfelt gratitude for knowing just what they needed to allow a deeper level of healing to reveal itself. Inevitably during the sharing portion of each class, numerous participants would recount that they'd felt Vision conducting healing work on them during the breathwork.

No matter how emotional or ungrounded someone was, Vision appeared unaffected, maintained his connection, and accepted them unconditionally. In fact, he seemed to seek out those with more frenetic energy as if on a mission to stabilize and ground them.

Star Wolf consistently received confirmation of Vision Wolf's ascended old soul status through well-known global intuitives and healers she met through her work. A famous Brazilian psychic medium invited Vision (and Star Wolf) to an intimate ceremonial gathering when he was nine months old. She relayed that Vision had had countless incarnations and forms. Another time, a Buddhist lama conveyed that Vision didn't have the soul of a dog, and that Vision had been a high lama in his most recent life. When Star Wolf inquired as to why Vision would incarnate as a dog after such a prestigious life, the lama shared in a matter-of-fact manner that embodying a dog was a very honorable incarnation as it teaches the master how to support someone else in becoming a master, while simultaneously allowing them to rest from all the responsibility and polarity typically experienced in a human body. Seneca Wolf Clan elder Grandmother Twylah Nitsch declared that Vision was a respected elder and welcomed him to eat with them at the table like her wolves had done in her home.

He was often invited to sacred ceremonies wherein dogs had never previously been allowed. Vision was always comfortable in these settings and was viewed as an equal to all those who had gathered together. From an early age, he didn't flinch while being smudged for the ceremony and wasn't affected by the drums or rattles.

He was always a gentleman who exuded kindness. His very presence conveyed unconditional love, and he unfailingly held Transformational Healing Presence. Star Wolf would often observe how Vision always gave his full attention to whoever was speaking to him. He respectfully listened with his whole heart while simultaneously being aware of his surroundings. He lived in a higher level of consciousness, which allowed him to easily navigate from his higher senses.

Around the time that they came into each other's lives, Star Wolf began a new cycle of her life and embarked on a deep transformational journey of death and rebirth, and love and loss. She delved into a period of time that was filled with transformative shadow work, soul integration, and purification. Star Wolf was catapulted into an escalated ascension process to embody 5D living and serve at greater levels than she knew she had the capacity to do. And Vision was right there beside her every step of the way. He empowered and supported her to do the necessary inner soul work so she could hold more light and be a wayshower for others. He was her familiar and their bond was undeniable. They spoke without speaking. And they were a formidable force of good in the world.

Through their seventeen-year powerful shamanic partnership, Star Wolf created and birthed her own vision for her service work to the world. She founded Venus Rising Association for Transformation, a nonprofit dedicated to healing and transformation for the planet, while simultaneously creating trademarked training and transformation programs including shamanic breathwork, a shamanic psychospiritual graduate school in North Carolina, and a shamanic-based spiritual community in the North Carolina mountains. Thousands of people from around the world have visited the community and gone through Star Wolf's programs.

When Star Wolf received clear guidance from Vision that he was ready to return "home" and was in his final hours, she sent out a prayer request on social media and to the residents of the community she had founded. Within an hour, thousands upon thousands of people from around the globe began sharing stories of how Vision had deeply touched their hearts and souls and changed them for the better. Vision received many visitors on his final day who were respectfully paying homage to him and expressing gratitude through Skype or in person. All who loved him went into prayer and held sacred space for his return to spirit.

In the exact moment of his veterinarian-assisted transition back to spirit, the song "Here Comes the Sun" by the Beatles suddenly began playing from Star Wolf's music playlist, which brought her much comfort. Star Wolf wrapped him in a blanket that Grandmother Twylah had gifted her, and several people helped to carry him to the burial site on the mountain behind their home. They prayed over him while holding hands, and then

Star Wolf asked out loud to the heavens, "Vision, give me a sign that you made it to the other side," and, in true Vision fashion, in that very moment a magnificent comet soared across the clear night sky. The group began howling in joy to honor this incredible soul and his amazing life!

Star Wolf has said that Vision was a gift from the Gods, and she doesn't know how she could have gotten through those deeply transformative and pivotal years without him. I'm certain Vision would reciprocate her feelings for they always mirrored each other. These two amazing luminaries will forever be bonded and united by their love. Vision helped Star Wolf to step into her role as a visionary and wayshower. Today she is a world renowned, deeply loved and respected shaman and leader. Her work continues to flourish and Vision Wolf lovingly supports her from another dimension. Star Wolf still senses his energy, and he often

Linda Star Wolf and Vision

Star Wolf and Vision in their early years together

visits her during dreamtime, reminding her that they will forever be connected and that their sacred service of the heart continues.

Aho, Star Wolf and Vision Wolf, for being exemplary examples of not playing small and shining your lights to birth a higher frequency of light and love on our beautiful planet!

---✳---

Transformational Soul Practice
Connecting with Your Soul Pack

Reflections: Journal your thoughts and observations of what this story has brought into your awareness for your growth. Seek the nugget or gift for you to embrace.

What part brought up the most emotion?
Can you see yourself or your animal in Star Wolf and Vision?
How have they inspired you?

Star Wolf and Vision teach the importance of community and serving a higher purpose to unearth a new time. Seek out like-minded beings who contribute to creating positivity and 5D experiences in your life.

Those you are seeking are seeking you. Whether this means intentional living or a new spiritual family or church, being around those that uplift and support us is imperative for our ascension into a higher dimension here on Earth.

- *Begin by visualizing the type of community or kindred spirits you want in your life and feel it in every fiber of your being.*
- *Trust the process and take actions steps as you feel guided.*
- *You can always call upon Vision Wolf to show you the way to connect with your soul pack!*

PART III

Your Sacred Work

Love is the recognition of oneness, sensing that you share the same consciousness.

ECKHART TOLLE

10

Ease Their Journey

Always remember, you have within you the strength, the patience, and the passion to reach for the stars to change the world.

HARRIET TUBMAN

Animals are often the glue that holds us and our families together. Over the years I have learned from domesticated animals that they're more than happy to lighten our physical and emotional loads through a multitude of ways. As your level of consciousness continues to expand, you will more easily recognize when your animal is actively working on you or is trying to awaken you to something that needs your attention. As you become more skilled at reaching for the higher purpose in their actions, their negative behavior will often stop on a dime and sometimes even a physical issue will "suddenly" be miraculously healed.

As you have almost certainly observed, our animals can often be sponges for our bottled-up emotions. Unlike most humans, animals do not have an illusion of separation. Their higher senses accurately detect any imbalances in our energy, and they instinctively begin serving us to restore harmony to our symbiotic relationship. They always know what we're thinking, feeling, and emotionally repressing, and they are wired to automatically relieve us of any discomfort. It is nothing short of extraordinary what they are willing to do for us.

At some point most animal lovers have said that there isn't anything they wouldn't do to help their animals feel better and suffer less. But what exactly does that mean? When I made that statement earlier in my life it meant that I would somehow find the money to do whatever was medically recommended to help my beloved animal companion feel better physically. But once I became aware of our sacred soul partnership my focus shifted to their emotional and spiritual wellness. When we raise our consciousness and begin looking at our animals as our teachers, guides, and wayshowers, we can no longer ignore their higher messages for our soul.

There is nothing worse than seeing our animal suffer, and our discomfort is exacerbated when we realize that it is often *our* energy that is negatively affecting them in some way. The good news is that we each have the ability to dramatically ease their burdens by making 5D choices for their well-being, and ours! When you consistently put in place higher vibrational habits and self-care, it allows an easier release of the protection around your emotional wounds, such that doing your inner work doesn't have to be some daunting, painful undertaking that you resist or avoid.

Your animal companions don't want you to bypass healing your own heart. In fact, they intentionally direct your focus to your personal growth because they recognize that this is the path to sustaining a higher frequency and feeling more love and less suffering. They want you to live your best life and have the same level of commitment to your inner growth and evolution as they do.

As conscious animal lovers, we can use this knowledge to motivate us to do the inner work and utilize their mirrors and guidance to bring about faster resolutions to all our life lessons. Over two decades ago, I realized that my soul deliberately partnered with my animal companions for a big portion of my personal growth, and I'm not alone! Millions of humans have willingly collaborated with animals and are now waking up to learn how infinitely intertwined our journeys are with these amazing creatures.

Your willingness to work on raising your vibration first has a positive ripple effect for your much-loved companions. This absolutely doesn't mean to stop tending to their physical needs. It instead proposes that when you become aware of how your energy affects them, you find the courage to put the oxygen mask on yourself first and observe your relationship from a higher perspective. And if you do this more often than not over the course of your time together, you will both reap the long-term benefits and live healthier, more meaningful lives.

Held within the soul contracts we planned with our animals are their undercover spiritual missions. These missions are always operating at a frequency that best serves our mutual evolution. Their negative behaviors and ailments are often beckoning you to dive deeper into a transformational shadow journey to heal your unresolved traumas, emotional wounds, and even your ancestral lineage. But how do you do that?

Throughout the pages that follow, I share guidance that is rooted in revealing how you and your animal kin can routinely live more joyous, peaceful, loving lives. My intention is to provide you with 5D tools, healthy habits, modalities, and rituals that can dramatically enhance your frequency and create the lasting shifts you so deserve.

As you begin to embrace more 5D practices you will rediscover a new level of the Divine presence within and create a meaningful, tranquil life for yourself and your animal companions. This path requires that you love yourself enough to begin to release resistance to allowing abundance to flow through every aspect of your life. And it also entails being kind and compassionate to yourself as you unravel and unlearn distorted beliefs that are no longer serving you.

Tuning into a 5D reality is the perfect kindling to fuel your forward progression to a higher frequency and boost your ability to anchor more light. Know that it is safe for you to rise above earthly suffering and embrace 5D consciousness on behalf of yourself, your animals, our planet, and the universe. The time is now to become the CEO of your own life!

11

Creating Habits and Rituals through 5D Practices

As we own our role as a member of this 5D team and increase our cellular frequency and continuously clear our emotional field, the part we are to play in the planetary transformation becomes clearer.

JUDITH CORVIN-BLACKBURN

Never before has there been a more opportune time to declare your intentions to embrace new ways to love yourself through making higher vibrational choices. Your soul will jump for joy when you put in place practices that benefit every aspect of your life! And the well-earned reward is that you will more frequently feel the glorious bliss of *oneness.* Furthermore, you will undoubtedly feel happier, healthier, and have a strong sense of Divine purpose in your heart. Through your intent to move up the vibrational ladder, you set in motion the unfolding and achievement of your soul's aspirations. The results of implementing these 5D frequency rituals will motivate you to continue down the glorious path to a higher state of consciousness.

You are so worthy of allowing in these high vibrational frequencies. Take a deep breath right now and declare to yourself and to the universe: *I am worthy of living in the tranquility and harmony of the fifth dimension.*

New habits require a foundation of self-love and self-mastery, but know that you are far from being alone on your journey from 3D to 5D. You are supported in your plan to embrace 5D living by all other beings that are already maintaining a higher frequency, like your animal companions! Their desire to ease your way to a higher dimension will comfort you like a warm blanket. Your Higher Self and your spiritual team of advisors that work with you in the spiritual realm are also championing your aspiration to move beyond polarity.

This is your time to give birth to a new way of being and living from your heart. Gift yourself the priority of tending to your own vibrational frequency so you will come to know how empowering it is to become the authority of your life.

As you read through my favorite 5D practices in the pages that follow, keep in the forefront of your mind that every new 5D habit you develop greatly benefits your animal kin. Be gentle with yourself as you break down distorted belief systems that are no longer serving you and release anything that is preventing a clear path to an easier way of living. Breathe into the new ways and love yourself through each and every experience. Look to your animal for validation that your new habits are perfectly unfolding for the betterment of you both. Also know that laughter, having a good sense of humor, and feeling joy are all magnificent 5D qualities!

GROUND YOUR INTENTIONS

It's always an excellent idea to set your intentions for changes and shifts you want to create in your life to embody an easier, more loving, and abundant fifth-dimensional life. To establish and decide on your intentions, you might want to sit in the stillness and call in your celestial spiritual advisors for support (animal and human!). Ask yourself: What are your deepest desires? How do you want to feel? What is most important to your soul as you embrace a higher frequency? Then write the answers down and place them on your altar or in another sacred location.

To reinforce your intentions, try creating a daily affirmation that grounds and supports your alignment with your desire to allow more 5D experiences. For example, on workdays, I often state: Divine Presence, help me to show up as my best self and align with serving more beings through rewarding work that I love. When I wholeheartedly declare my intentions for the day, I can feel the alignment in my body.

After you state your affirmation, be sure to take several deep breaths, and then visualize your affirmation as reality to activate it in your heart. Then the universe instinctively and enthusiastically responds in kind by whispering "Yes! We support you!" Putting this practice into effect each day energetically sets the course for how your day unfolds. Additional examples of affirmations include:

- My intention is to embody 5D habits and live vibrantly in a higher frequency of love.
- Today will be a high frequency, positive day!
- My intention is to live a more expansive and happy life!

- I give myself permission to have a joy-filled, abundant, and productive day.
- I seek the higher purpose and gifts held within each experience and lean into 5D living with ease and grace.
- I am grounded and aware of the magic that is always around me.

VIBRATIONAL AWARENESS

Maintaining your vibrational frequency is of the utmost importance in allowing more loving 5D experiences. Feeling good matters, a lot, and making conscious choices that support your desire to enhance your vibrational well-being is music to your soul's ears. Everything has a vibrational frequency, and this includes words, food, books, music, movies, social media posts, and you! Since your vibration dictates your experiences, it's wise to look at your choices. Take stock of what you read, watch, or listen to, and if there is more of a 3D duality or violence theme, you might want to take a step back and consider shifting to options that lift you up.

Keep your power by opting for what feels right for you. As frequently as possible, love yourself enough to make choices that enhance your vibrational frequency. You can be aware of current events without being triggered into a lower dimension. When you feel triggered by something, detach, breathe into your heart, and intentionally connect to a higher power, your Higher Self, or simply a higher frequency of love. Triggers are merely indications that there is something going on within you that needs to be healed and released in healthy ways.

The higher you are vibrating, the less tolerant your system

will be to allowing in lower frequency experiences. Everyone is different in what they are able to endure while still maintaining the vibration they desire, so listen to the wisdom of your heart for guidance.

BUILD YOUR OBSERVER MUSCLE

Becoming adept at observing your choices, thoughts, and reactions is essential to develop healthy 5D habits. In one of my favorite spiritual books, *The Untethered Soul,* author Michael Singer writes about creating a "lucid self" wherein you become aware of your thoughts but are not immersed in them. Others might refer to a similar concept as the "observer self." I believe the ability to detach from the emotional entanglement of our thoughts and shift to observing them opens the gateway to connect more intimately with our Higher Self. Building our internal observer muscle is a crucial component in the process of our ascension to 5D living.

Your thoughts and emotional reactions to situations are often the very cause of your emotional and physical distress. We've all had those moments when we ask ourselves: Why did I react that way? Why did I say that? While your observer self says: Oh, I can see I am reacting from a place of wounding. There's something here for me to look at more intimately so I can heal it from within and allow the deeper wounding to heal and release.

As 3D humans, we tend to give way too much real estate in our thoughts to unfounded fears and what I call internal conspiracy theories. Our thoughts often run rampant with the "what ifs," so much so that you begin believing in something that will never actually come to fruition. These fears and stories we create can cause stress, worry, anxiety, sleepless nights, and even physical manifestations.

Begin to intentionally use your thoughts to manifest more positivity in your body, and in your life, by focusing on what you want to feel, be, and do. When you catch yourself going down a rabbit hole of worry, or you are about to give voice to your usual reaction (that has likely never brought about your desired outcome), detach from the situation by taking several deep breaths directly into your heart and then shift into your observer self. Speak kindly to the part of yourself that is having the emotional reaction, as if you were lovingly speaking to a child or animal to calm their fears. Hitting the pause button when you are in the middle of an internal or external reaction can aid in allowing the feelings to move through you without being enmeshed in a lower dimensional reactive pattern.

You have the ability within you to master your thoughts and can choose to begin cleaning out the closet of your distorted beliefs to give your fears the boot. As with any new habit, it takes practice to perfect, so pat yourself on the back when you are able to detach and observe your reactions from a higher perspective. This keeps you out of polarity and in a position of 5D power.

GRATITUDE GALORE!

There is not a more effective practice to raise your vibration faster than feeling heartfelt gratitude. It has the ability to catapult you into a state of feeling immeasurably blessed. When you feel genuine gratitude so much that your heart opens and tears well up in your eyes, you are swimming in a 5D oasis pool of love unlike any other!

Open a portal of gratitude in your heart and seek out reasons to be grateful. Once you get in the habit of finding the blessings in each experience, the universe conspires to send you more reasons to be grateful.

After I get into bed each night, the last thing I do before falling asleep is express gratitude for at least three things that happened that day. It usually ends up being many more than three because once we move our focus to our blessings, it's easier to see them! On challenging days, it's even more important to find the gifts to elevate your vibration. Many have found that a daily gratitude journal aids in their intention to count their blessings.

Whatever rituals you create to tap into the vibration of gratitude, you are sure to see the benefits. Engage in giving and receiving gratitude at every available opportunity, and you will quickly see the positive changes it creates in your life.

THE SPIRITUAL SUPERPOWERS

Out of the seemingly endless fifth-dimensional virtues that are available, I'm placing specific emphasis on acceptance (lack of judgment), compassion, and forgiveness. Practiced routinely, these three qualities will propel you into 5D living and bring about deep transformation for yourself and all other beings that you touch with your light. Most domesticated animals have mastered these qualities, so follow their lead.

The not-so-hidden gift of these virtues is how they each are beckoning you to raise your awareness and recognize that for them to work their magic in the world, you must first shower yourself with them: Your acceptance of others reflects the depth of acceptance of the self. Your compassion for others reflects the depth of compassion for the self. Your forgiveness of others reflects the depth of forgiveness of the self.

If you find yourself struggling with expressing any of these superpower virtues, look within to discover what part of yourself needs acceptance, compassion, or forgiveness. Then give yourself an abundance of that virtue to free yourself from the chains of 3D wounding and ease your way into a deeper connection with the Divine. Make it a habit to look inward at your needs for these virtues, as this will more quickly aid in your ability to do the same with others.

Self-blame creates an energetic armory that holds others at a distance. You are worthy of shifting the old programming and creating healthier self-talk habits to consciously create a deeper level of grace and peace within. So lavish acceptance, compassion, and forgiveness upon yourself and all those you meet along your journey, and notice how much better you feel.

THE ULTIMATE 5D HABIT: LOVING YOURSELF

When you regularly implement the aforementioned spiritual superpowers, you light the way to dramatically enhance your ability to love yourself. And this, my friend, is the life-changing attribute that will completely transform your lack and victim consciousness into living an abundant life filled with miracles and magic. Self-love precipitates the inner knowing that you are lovable, that you matter, and that you are a brilliant, beautiful spark of the Divine. Loving yourself also fosters the sharing of your innate Divine gifts in the manner your soul designed.

There are many souls that incarnate into human form with a main objective of learning how to love themselves unconditionally. In addition, there are many that preplanned (at a soul level) to remain single for much of their life to intentionally engage in a journey of self-love and service.

Sometimes people haven't experienced being unconditionally loved except by an animal. We often contract with them to show us this quality so we can experience the frequency of unconditional love firsthand. Integrating our animal's teachings are key to knowing how to love ourselves.

In our society it can be challenging to fully love ourselves because of the prevalent 3D focus on material goods and physical appearances. Nevertheless, it is a life-defining moment when we are able to grasp the concept of loving ourselves and, in turn, begin shutting down the harmful inner critic. What a beautiful moment it is when you realize that the safest place you can live is in the sanctuary of your heart.

CREATIVE EXPRESSION

You are meant to create beautiful blessings in the world with your unique skills. You can create for personal pleasure, for the Earth, or for sharing something with the world. The frequency of the fifth dimension is ripe for the flow of creating. In fact, this is one of your barometers for knowing when you are tapping into 5D consciousness. Every time you are creating something to share with the world from your heart you are simultaneously birthing something new within yourself.

When you are gardening, painting, writing, or building something, you are beautifully tethered into a fifth-dimensional frequency. In addition, when you are joyfully creating, your body automatically releases a plethora of the feel-good hormones dopamine and oxytocin. You might notice that as your vibration increases, more and more ideas that you feel drawn to create will pop into your heart and mind. This is because creating feels both purposeful and pleasurable! So give yourself permission to carve out time to let your 5D creative juices flow, and feel joy throughout the process.

LEAN INTO SPIRITUAL SUPPORT

Much like your animal companions, the universe has your back and is always conspiring to support you by way of organically responding to your vibration. There are infinite ways your celestial light team of advisors can and will provide assistance to your every need on your evolutionary journey. When you peel back the layers of protection around your heart and connect more intimately with the Divine, you create a level of faith that weathers every storm. This newfound faith in yourself and the universe allows a higher frequency of spiritual support to flow throughout your day-to-day life.

It's beneficial for us to work on healing any feelings of unworthiness as soon as we observe them operating in our psyche, as this might inadvertently keep our desired outcomes in vibrational escrow for a longer period of time. However, despite our 3D fears and resistance, if we consistently nurture our spiritual connection, "good stuff" still lands squarely on the doorstep of our hearts.

Your spirit guides, or angels, are always eager to champion you in the fulfillment of your soul's plan. They instantly respond to your reactions and needs and, if need be, will send you messages through a gamut of ways. Their guidance might arrive via the symbolism of your animals' actions, signs, song lyrics, nature, or your dreams, to name a few.

While I was preparing to write this book, there was a period of time that I was feeling very overwhelmed. Then one night, I had a dream that completely shifted my outlook, brought a huge smile to my heart, and reinforced the knowing that I am never alone.

In the dream I was distraught because I'd suddenly discovered that my car had been crashed and I'd lost my keys and phone. I began frantically walking up narrow pathways of stairs between buildings and going through many white doors. Then I noticed that a couple had lodged a long wooden stick into one of the doors to secure it and ensure that the "bad guys" were restrained from getting to us. As I stood looking at the door, it suddenly burst open. Behind the door was the brilliant vision of the entire universe, and about seven or eight smiling young men with magical wings, hovering in space and looking directly at me. The closest young man said, "We're with the International Rescue Group, and we're here to support you. The woman who caused the accident with your car started a crowd funding campaign, and it has been exponentially growing via donations from people all over the world. All is well!" Then out of nowhere someone handed over my phone, along with a sparkling brand-new car key.

Upon awakening and remembering this fabulous dream, it catapulted me into a higher dimension such that my fears dissipated, and I knew without a doubt that everything would be just fine. Dreams are a valuable tool to guide your journey and receive pure messages from your Higher Self and light team. Because of this dream, when I feel lost and scared, I remind myself that the International Rescue Group will blast through my fears to support me! And the good news is that you also have a myriad of spiritual support and your very own International Rescue Group to lean into through each and every experience and project you embark upon.

Make an intention to intimately connect heart-to-heart to the beings of light that are always there to support you and light your pathway to the next dimension of consciousness.

MEDITATION RITUAL

The benefits of creating a meditation practice are endless. It's one of the highest vibrational habits you can implement into your daily routine. This sacred ritual can be utilized to get grounded, connected, healed, or cleared, to raise your frequency, and even to enhance your intuition. Meditation is also a marvelous way to garner self-love and connect with the pure essence of your soul. This essence, the real you, holds the key to embodying more fifth-dimensional experiences.

Whatever amount of time you carve out to meditate, render it your sacred time to become one with the highest aspect of yourself. If you have developed your higher senses, while meditating you might observe or feel energy and emotions releasing and a higher vibration of light pouring into your energy field.

There is a plethora of different ways to meditate, including a variety of more formal methods, for which the internet is a wonderful source. Follow your intuition to find the right and perfect meditation ritual for you and your lifestyle. It's not a chore; it's a spiritual gift to yourself. The goal is to find a meditation ritual that soothes your soul such that you experience it as time well spent.

I really enjoy the daily use of a meditation app because I appreciate having the singing bowl timer chimes and options of soft background sounds or chanting. Sometimes a guided meditation can be helpful to keep your mind focused and engaged. There are many guided meditations available. I've created a variety of guided meditations that are available for free to help you to heal emotional wounds and enhance your level of self-love. (See p. 232 for more information.)

Meditation Ritual Suggestions

1. Create an altar that includes several sacred element pieces to reflect your intention for your ritual.

2. Begin your meditation with an invocation that calls upon your spiritual allies to join you.

3. Visualize a strong boundary of light around you that serves as protection and creates a vessel of purification of the highest vibration imaginable.

4. Telepathically invite your animal friends to join you. Some animals prefer to be with you physically, while others would rather remain in another room. Honor their choice.

5. State a prayer, affirmation, or intention for your meditation time. Perhaps prepare a few to use, and then see what serves you best in that moment.

6. State any additional intentions or requests from your

light team. Sometimes I'll say: Help me to free my body, mind, and soul of anything that is not supporting me so I can become a 5D bridge from heaven to Earth.

7. Get comfortable and relax your body, including your jaw, neck, shoulders, and arms.

8. Take several deep breaths to calm your body, mind, and soul as you invite in a higher vibration of light to fill you.

9. Bring your attention to your heart and breathe into it. If you feel so guided, perhaps place your hands in prayer pose or directly on your heart.

10. If thoughts pop into your mind, visualize them being air-lifted out of your energy field. Then bring your attention back to your heart and the breath.

11. Always close your meditation time in prayer pose, if possible, and express gratitude to all those that collaborated with you for your highest and best.

CONSCIOUSLY CONSUME

We are spiritually growing such that our very being is preparing itself to expand and ground more light. Because of this, consciously or unconsciously, people are becoming more aware of what they consume and how it directly affects their vibration. Farm-to-table restaurants are popping up everywhere, and there are more farmers markets and brick-and-mortar locations for healthier food and supplements than ever before.

You will find that the higher the frequency you are maintaining, the less tolerant your body might be of medicines, processed foods, gluten, sugar, dairy, caffeine, and alcohol. Everything you put in your body has a vibrational frequency that affects your physical temple and your energy field. Before you consume anything, it is wise to purify and bless it, fill it with light, and visualize it moving through your body with ease and grace. Be sure to include the water you drink and use in cooking. And always express gratitude for everything you ingest to further foster well-being in your body.

Food is often a tool to (unconsciously) repress our emotions or numb us, which doesn't support our long-term goal of raising our frequency. Aspire to feed yourself what truly nourishes you—and for example, your self-love and superpower virtues I mentioned earlier—which simultaneously increases your capacity to nourish others. Home grown or locally grown organic food has the highest vibration that will best serve your physical temple. Make an intention to make conscious choices about what you consume, but give yourself permission to start where you are and do the best you can.

BODY TEMPLE LOVE

Our bodies are the most incredible gifts! The body's magnificent design substantiates that there is a collaborative brilliant mind behind its creation. Sometimes we take our body for granted and resist giving it the TLC it so deserves. Taking good care of our physical temples is a form of self-love. Our bodies need daily stretching and movement to release emotions and energetic attachments, get grounded and connected to Mother Earth, and create a favorable environment to maintain a high state of wellness.

Find an activity that you enjoy so it doesn't feel like a chore. Do what makes your soul happy, and the energy will carry you from there. Dancing is a wonderful option to move your body and feel pleasure. Perhaps seek out others that enjoy similar kinds of movement, like your animal companion! Hiking, sports, exercise groups, or any other activity that you are keen on will also allow for a more natural unfolding of the habit to ensue. You might want to engage with a healing practitioner to ensure that your body is in alignment.

Ensuring that your body receives enough sleep is a crucial component for almost every earthly thing you want to do each day. Sleep affects everything! Create a high-vibrational sleep environment. I highly recommend a "no electronics" rule for your bedroom. The energy that emanates from televisions and phones negatively affects the vibration of what should be the most peaceful room in your home. Before you doze off at night, visualize and create a sacred force field of light and love surrounding your bed in all directions. You can also put crystals with protective and cleansing properties in the corners of your bedroom to create a grid of safety to induce a calm, regenerative sleep.

Many of us have nighttime childhood (or adult) traumas that can unconsciously contribute to disturbing our sleep. It's important to intentionally establish a safe haven that encourages a restful, deep sleep. I've found that meditating for five minutes at bedtime can still the mind and allow an easier launch into dreamtime.

Express appreciation for your extraordinary body temple, for it has been through much and has transported you through many experiences. As you learn to respect your body and treat it with utmost kindness, you will naturally feel guided to give it what it really yearns for to maintain a frequency of well-being.

COMMUNE WITH NATURE

Nature is a remarkable healer that will revitalize your very essence at its core. I cannot think of a more effortless way to connect to the oneness of a higher consciousness than spending time in nature. The purity of Mother Earth and all of her inhabitants helps us to connect to our true nature. Whether you are at the beach, on a mountain or a rock, or sitting in your garden, make an intention to commune and connect with your surroundings, and drink in the energy of Mama Gaia.

Every plant, tree, and flower is showing us how to grow and evolve by living within the oneness of spirit. Everything in nature has an authentic and symbiotic relationship with other elements for survival. In addition, the universe organically utilizes nature to send us messages in our highest and best.

Your animals are well aware of nature's innate regenerative abilities. They instinctively seek to utilize the gifts of Mother Earth, Father Sky, the sun, and the moon for their well-being. We are also wired with a similar inherent need to source solace and connection through the oneness of spending time in our favorite outdoor setting. Seek communion with Mother Earth and allow her grounding, peaceful spirit to comfort, console, and reassure you that, indeed, all is well.

IMPLEMENTING YOUR 5D HABITS
AND RITUALS

It is truly possible to feel harmony and tranquility in our day-to-day lifestyle here on Earth! To begin with, set reasonable expectations for your new practices and aim for 5D moments, then for 5D hours. The goal is to live authentically and dismantle the inner critic, so take things at the pace of the most wounded part of yourself. You will recognize when you are moving up in vibration because your typical triggers will not be as charged, and you'll have a stronger sense of trust, faith, and connection. Rest assured that you and your spiritual team of advisors can handle whatever curveballs come your way. Like a flower, you will instinctively grow toward the light to meet the needs for your soul expressions in the world.

12

5D Healing Modalities for People and Animals

Sound will be the medicine of the future.

EDGAR CAYCE

During Raglan's first check-up the rescue center's veterinarian discovered that the beautiful feline was completely deaf. For the most part, she kept to herself after integrating with the other cats in the Good Mews Animal Foundations free-roaming cat room. Volunteers and potential adopters couldn't help but notice that any affection she shared with others was strictly on her terms, which equated into her being overlooked on adoption days. Raglan didn't lay out the welcome mat to her heart easily and would often lash out at those wanting to shower her with love and affection.

However, every time vibrational sound therapist Michael Burke facilitated a sound journey group for the cats and the two-legged attendees, Raglan turned into a friendly, affectionate, and loving cat. The musical sounds spoke her language through the vibration of the instruments Michael played.

Michael recalls an extraordinarily heart-opening experience with Raglan while playing the flute during one of his sound journeys. Raglan was resting on the cat tree behind him when she was suddenly drawn to the soothing vibrations of the flute. She climbed onto his shoulder, sat down, and then gently and intentionally moved her head down within inches of the flute. How wonderful, Michael thought, that this beautiful cat can energetically feel the soothing and comforting sounds. Then Michael felt the emotional reaction from Raglan's beautiful soul through energy transference and, for a moment, their souls merged. He was moved to tears because he could feel her gratitude and excitement for the experience.

It's validating to see such a palpable response from an animal relying solely on its higher senses. If Raglan responds so positively to the sacred sounds and vibrations, wouldn't they also be beneficial to humans? Given that there is virtually no placebo effect with animals, this is another great example of how they are showing us the way to respond from our hearts and how to naturally gravitate to the higher frequencies to utilize their healing properties.

Animals will instinctively be drawn toward what will best serve their well-being. And you can count on them to let you know their desires and preferences *if* you are aware of how to detect and read their reactions. Every time I took my cat companion MaiTai to receive a chiropractic adjustment, he would always let the veterinarian know the exact place he was out of alignment. She used a pendulum to determine the locations of where he needed to be adjusted by moving it above his spine as he lay on her table. Unfailingly, he would turn sharply to look at her when the pendulum was over a particular spot as if saying "right there!"

Humans have the same ability to distinguish and intuit

which healing method will serve their highest and best. We are all uniquely wired and will respond differently to each and every mode of healing. The end-all-be-all healing approach for one person may not serve the next person or animal in the same manner. When you regularly maintain a higher level of consciousness, it's easier to tap into your internal guidance system to discern what's right for you, and trust that others can do the same for themselves.

There are many types of alternative and holistic healing methods designed to help you raise your frequency to restore health to your body and energy field and simultaneously get you connected to the expansiveness of a higher stream of consciousness. In chapter 8 you read about Elaine's challenging childhood and how her perspective on life began improving after regularly attending a yoga class in college. This demonstrates the powerful effects of utilizing a 5D healing modality that simultaneously works with our bodies *and* our energy fields.

If you've read my previous books or if we have worked together, you already know that energy healing radically changed my life such that I no longer needed the eight daily medications I thought I'd be taking forever. Because of the miraculous and tangible results I received in my body, I attended four years of training and supervision to become certified in the trade. Now I am fortunate to help others expedite their inner emotional healing journey to gently release their emotional wounds and create a healthier environment for their bodies to heal. When we personally experience and feel the changes in ourselves, it instills a desire to help others do the same. Engaging in a dedicated inner healing journey utilizing gentler ways of healing can be life-changing and can accelerate our ascension to higher dimensional living.

There are myriad alternative healing options that it would behoove you to explore, for yourself and your animal, to boost your ascension to the fifth dimension. They all serve the purpose of helping you to lighten your load without the use of invasive chemicals or surgeries. Know that I am absolutely not suggesting that you forego the use of mainstream medical treatments, for they also provide a wonderful service and sometimes are the best choice for your well-being.

5D Healing Modalities

The following are various types of 5D modalities that I suggest researching to discern if any are fitting for your health objectives. Most of these options are also available for animals! This is not a complete list of alternative and holistic modalities, but they are the ones I am familiar with enough to feel comfortable recommending.

Acupuncture	Healing with herbs
Ayurveda	Homeopathy
Breathwork	Jin Shin Jyutsu
Chinese medicine	Massage therapy
Chiropractic	Qi Gong
CranioSacral	Reflexology
Crystal therapy	Shiatsu
Emotional Freedom	Sound therapy
Technique (also known as	Tai Chi
EFT, or Tapping)	Underwater therapy
Energy healing	Yoga

The design of our energy fields is extraordinary and complex in nature. Similar to our bodies, they are perpetually, consistently seeking equilibrium to return to their natural state of wellness. When we utilize a holistic 5D healing modality as part of our wellness routine, we are organically tending to our energy field to release any energetic and emotional congestion. Left unreleased, our repressed energy and emotions will set up shop somewhere in our body and potentially manifest into a physical ailment or issue. Hence the importance of tending to both our body *and* our energy field to induce a healthy environment to allow them to do what they are designed to do: heal themselves.

While it is critical that you choose a modality that best suits you and your lifestyle, it is equally important that you resonate with the energy of the practitioner, doctor, facilitator, or instructor. It's crucial that *their* energy be as clear as possible because it dramatically contributes to the effectiveness of their work. The higher their vibration, the more you will benefit from partnering with them.

Healers and practitioners who are more frequently aligned with 5D consciousness will realize the importance of having integrity at the center of their practice. They are the conduit that will be holding sacred space for your healing journey to unfold. A 5D healer will always guide and empower you to listen to your own heart, for this is the fastest route to receiving the long-term wellness you seek. Hopefully, the practitioners are actively embodying 5D rituals, practices, and healing modalities themselves. Trust your heart to guide you to the right and perfect modality and person. The most reliable source of information is your own intuition.

Tips for Identifying the Best Energy Practitioner for You and/or Your Animals

1. Ask them about their background, training certifications, and how long they have been in practice.
2. Look at their online presence and read the testimonials. Do you resonate with and like what you see?
3. Your sessions will be much more productive if the healer has a clear connection to spirit and is as healthy as possible. Alcohol, drugs or medications, and even unhealthy eating habits can negatively affect the healer's vibration and connection. You'll get a sense of their energy when you speak with them.
4. Trust your gut. Do they feel like someone you can trust with your well-being? With your animals? Do you feel comfortable and safe in their presence to reveal even the parts of yourself that you judge? That's what is needed for you to begin a deeper healing journey and to truly begin releasing your inner core emotional wounds.
5. Inquire if they also work with a healer to get cleared and/or mentored. Have they themselves embarked on an inner healing journey to clear their energy and emotional wounds?
6. Do they walk their talk? If the answer is yes, they are likely living and working in integrity and are qualified to help you or your animal companion heal.
7. Commit to the healer and your inner healing journey. Once you find someone you feel safe with and trust it is a gift to your soul to find the courage to commit to the beautiful unfolding of your healing journey.

Let's take a deeper look at the healing benefits of two 5D modalities that have been traced back millions of years to the continents of Lemuria and the golden age of Atlantis: crystal therapy and sound therapy. Those that lived during that time apparently were able to maintain a fifth-dimensional frequency and have much to teach us as our planet continues its course toward a similar way of living. Since I do not consider myself proficient to teach about crystal and sound therapy, I contacted experts in these fields. I'm excited to share their wisdom with you!

SOUND THERAPY

The true masters of sacred sound therapy are the whales and dolphins. Because of their ability to maintain a high vibration, we are magically drawn to their mystical presence. Perhaps it is their use of sound that helps them to maintain a higher frequency, but there is so much more to their work than the fact that they are amazing creatures. I will always remember the first time I "met" a whale. The incredible humpback calmly surfaced within a few feet of our small boat off the coast of Mexico. I recall that suddenly everything got very still, as if time were slowing down so we wouldn't miss the magic. We each knew it was a sacred moment that we would forever treasure as the whale lingered for some time, gracing us with its presence. I recall sensing that the whale was filling us with Divine light, which immediately brought tears of gratitude, as it still does today.

A more esoteric belief is that the whales are intentionally creating and sending out specific vibrations that have the ability to keep the Earth's energy grid in a healthy state. The whales consider themselves a mirror of potential reflecting the higher consciousness that is available to each of us, according to those who claim to communicate with and channel the consciousness of whales. They also assert that they work with the Earth's grid lines, meridians, and energy fields to ensure unity among all life-forms.

There is a conscious movement transpiring in the West to raise awareness about the healing and soothing capabilities of the sacred sounds of different instruments, which produce a natural healing effect for all beings. This sacred work also beautifully mimics and expands the important work of the whales and dolphins.

Sound therapist Michael Burke was moved by Raglan, the deaf kitty, and her reaction to the sounds of his instruments, but he wasn't necessarily surprised. During his fifteen years of facilitating sacred sound journeys, Michael has consistently found that animals unequivocally gravitate to the healing sounds. When he volunteers his time to create sound journeys for the cats (and people) at Good Mews, frequently the felines will snuggle up in one of the crystal or Tibetan bowls. While Michael is playing, the feline attendees are consistently calm and will sink deeply into the soothing sounds. They instinctively take advantage of the healing energy that sound therapy provides by soaking up the vibrations and allowing the energy to beautifully restabilize their energy fields and bodies.

Michael's important and rewarding work facilitating sound journeys, also known as sound baths or sound immersions, has provided healing to thousands. Sound journeys help people to gently release traumas, emotional wounds, release

Michael Burke and Ollie Kitty at
Good Mews Animal Foundation

Michael's setup at the Good Mews Animal Foundation

and clear their energy fields, and strengthen their ability to hold and ground more light. Michael's dedication to helping others through sacred sound has taken his work to the fields of addiction and recovery, PTSD, and mental health. For many years he has been contracted by four different addiction, detox, and treatment centers to conduct sound journeys to ease their patient's recoveries. At these facilities, the employees and patients lovingly call him "Dr. Sound." Frequently those that journey with Michael are completely transformed through his work and will share how impactful the sound therapy has been to their revitalization. He recalls one gentleman stating after his first class, "I don't know what you just did, but I've never felt this good without a substance."

For seven years, I facilitated the spiritual community of Unity North Atlanta's (spiritual community) Praying Paws

Animal Service that people attended with their animals. This fun monthly service provided an animal-related spiritual message, prayer, meditation, song, and remembrance. I always asked one or two sound practitioners from their sacred sound ministry to arrive early to cleanse and purify the energy in the room through the sounds and vibrations from the bowls, and to also play during opening prayer to get the attendees grounded, connected, and in the present moment. It was fascinating how the bowls would magically induce a state of peaceful tranquility within the animals and their people.

CNN caught wind of the service and wanted to film a segment for their show *The Daily Share*. After the service attended by the CNN crew, I was interviewed by the producer and was surprised that she brought up the fact that all the animals were so calm, as if it was odd behavior. I could tell there was a bit of disappointment in her voice, as if she'd hoped for a bit more of a chaotic atmosphere to film. Instead, she said it felt as if they were attending a Zen service for animals. That's when I pointed out the sound practitioners and explained how the sounds had soothed and calmed the animals. That portion of the interview unfortunately didn't make the final cut that aired.

To understand more about the benefits of sound healing and how it actually works, I contacted world-renowned sacred sound shaman Don Reed Simmons. Don knows a thing or two about sacred sound. He's been the president of the International Sound Therapy Association (ISTA) for eleven years, facilitates the annual Global Cymatics Conference, and has been the go-to teacher of sound therapy in the southeastern United States and for countless people around the world. He's had a personal sound practice for decades, in addition to having established several sound ministries at spiritual centers, and he has trained hundreds of sound practitioners.

I've been fortunate to experience Don's incredibly powerful work on many occasions and knew he was the perfect person to provide answers to my questions about sound healing for people and animals. I don't know anyone more knowledgeable on the subject. Don's not only an expert on sound therapy, he's a huge animal lover!

Following are the questions I asked Don about sound therapy and his incredibly informative responses.

INTERVIEW WITH DON REED SIMMONS

Q: What is sound therapy?

Don: Sound is defined as the "oscillation in pressure, stress, particle displacement, and particle velocity" that creates an auditory experience. Sound therapy is bringing together vibrational pulse, tempo, and pitch in order to create harmony in the body, mind, and spirit. Sound therapy, as an ancient technique, has not changed that much, only the instruments used. Today a sound therapist might use a tuning fork, a two-prong acoustic resonator made of steel, nickel, and chromium, which can be tuned to different frequencies. Today you can also find tuning forks made of high-quality quartz crystal that are specifically tuned to different frequencies. A thousand years ago the shaman, a male or female spiritual practitioner of the tribe or community who is believed to interact with the spirit world and who facilitated healing, would have used a reed from the grass cupped in his or her hands creating a whistling effect. Or they may howl like a wolf, growl like a bear, or create a guttural sound to emulate the sound of a panther in order to infuse their patients with the Spirit of the animal. All of this is technically sound therapy.

Q: How does sound therapy heal?

Don: For healing purposes, sound is a vibrational tool to be used, like a pitch-pipe for a musical instrument, by which matter becomes aligned into the vibrational tone of the sound instrument. Everything, including organs, muscles, and bones of the body, has a vibrational "tone." By applying vibrational sound to the body, the body becomes realigned to the harmony of the tones placed upon it. When a sound instrument touches the body, or even comes in close contact, the flesh responds like the skin of a drum. We know skin is the largest organ on the body, and so as the skin begins to resonate with the appropriate sound from a therapist, this sound travels throughout the body topically as well as internally. Sound waves, the vibrational oscillation of sound, can penetrate deep into the human body, including organs, tissues, and even bones. Remember, the body is made up disproportionally of fluid, and fluid is a great conductor of sound. So when sound is introduced onto or around the body, the body responds automatically. You cannot help it. That's why it's so important to be aware of your surroundings and to really know the sound therapist you are working with. Anyone can bang a gong but only a few people know how to purposefully use a gong for healing. The vibrational shock wave, if used improperly, can be damaging not only to the ears and eardrums, but can also cause unwanted experiences like anger, fatigue, muscle soreness, and even bruising and tearing of tissue in the eyes and internal organs. Sound, as experienced by the military around the world, can also cause great damage. It was just a few years ago that several diplomats and American officials were suspected of being sonically attacked in Cuba, Russia, and China. To use sound as healing is to create a landscape of tonal qualities relating to health, well-being, and joy.

I have found animals are particularly susceptible to sound healing as they are uniquely designed for hearing and "feeling" the threats from nature. The animal kingdom at large, from the largest elephant to the tiniest kitten, are "in tune" with their surroundings, no pun intended, because they literally "tune in" to their surroundings to discern the different sounds around them. With many animals, their hearing is better than their vision. You can watch cats twitch their ears back, forth, and sideways, picking up the sounds around them. By angling their ears, they are picking up sound frequencies far beyond the range of human hearing. Elephants communicate with each other miles away by picking up a vibrational pulse from the bottom of their flat feet. Whales, through their clicks and whistles, send sound up to ten miles away to determine where they are, called echolocation, and to communicate with others their path of travel.

My friend Tina had a husky mix pup (not sure with what, we think wolf) from Sitka, Alaska, who came into my life when he was around five years old. Sitka loved sound therapy and would get up from wherever he was as soon as I picked up the gong and follow me, as he knew a session

206 * Your Sacred Work

was about to begin. He would lay down in close proximity to where the action was happening and just let the sound wash over him. Sitka was not a "lay at your feet" kind of dog, as many huskies are. They can be aloof, but several times when we used the Acoustic Meridian Intelligence (AMI) he would lay down with his head almost on top of our feet. The AMI is used as a healing tool, and I think that when he was not feeling good this was his way of "going to the doctor." In his older age, Tina would use tuning forks to help his arthritis and fatigue.

Q: What's the best way for a beginner to use sound on their healing journey?

Don: Sound therapy is really available to everyone and anyone. I like to begin teaching sound therapy by getting people to hum and feel the vibration in their chest. This sound and vibration brings us back to ourselves and creates a "grounding effect." I learned this by growing up on a farm around many cows. The sound of their mooing was like a beacon of sound saying "here I am." As a teenager I had to have a pretty serious surgery, and late one night, slightly afraid of what was to become of my situation, I felt this rising sound from deep within my chest. A long "mooooooo" emerged, and almost immediately I felt safe, as I could feel my body, still alive. So, start with the sound of your voice. Use modulation, pitch, and tempo, and just play around with your own voice and really feel how it resonates within your own body. The human body is like a drum, and it has a resonant sound to it. Begin to gently tap your chest and you will hear the sound of the drum.

Closing your eyes, you will find a rhythm to the drumbeat of what feels right to you. And this is key. What is right for you? It doesn't matter if you cannot sing or stay on key or keep rhythm with someone else. This is about you. What key you sing in is uniquely you. There is no wrong key when you are singing yourself. If someone says "you are off key," just tell them you are a solo artist and not fit for the chorus!

When someone wants to have an instrument, a Himalayan bowl is what I recommend first as it is metal, so it's hard to break, and it's easy to use. Just gently tap. Gently tap. Even a Himalayan bowl can become obnoxious if not played properly. It helps when you align your breathing to the sound of the tap. Meditation and sound go hand in hand. If you have difficulty in making the bowl sing or if your tapping is out of sync, it's because you, the practitioner, are out of sync. Before I play anything, I do a quick one-minute meditation holding the bowl or mallet to make the connection between my personal rhythms of breathing and the instruments before me. This is why many people in meditation use this style bowl. I would also suggest everyone have a tuning fork in his or her medicine chest. Here, unfortunately, money does matter. It comes down to the quality of the tuning fork and the precision it is made. The recommended tuning fork would be either an Otto 128 (weighted), to stimulate the nervous system and improve circulation, or the OM fork (weighted) at 136.1 Hz, which is the cosmic sound OM, a sound chanted by the ancient yogis and modern meditators alike. The Otto 128 stimulates and awakens the body while the OM fork calms down and relieves stress on the body.

John Beaulieu, N.D., Ph.D. is one of the best practitioners and teachers of tuning forks, and the quality of his forks are excellent. His book *Human Tuning* is a staple in the bookshelf of every sound therapist I know.

Eileen Day McKusick is another person whose book, *Tuning the Human Biofield,* is another staple of sound therapy. Her tuning forks and teachings are also excellent.

Rattles have been used for centuries by ancient shamans and modern sound healers alike. There are fancy rattles you can purchase, or you can make your own by putting a few rocks or rice in a container. You can even use the keys you carry in your purse or pocket or even a half-filled Tic Tac container to create a rattle sound. Close your eyes and let the rhythm come to you as you listen to what feels right that is compassionate, loving, and healing.

Q: Is there a way for people to locate a sound therapist in their area?

Don: Sound therapists are, unfortunately, not a registered group. The International Sound Therapy Association (ISTA) is currently working on bringing that into fruition as a governing body in order to have a standard of quality around the world. Many people are teaching and facilitating sound therapy, but not all are the same. There is no "body of quality," so you really have to experience the person and teaching to feel if it is right for you. Don't be fooled by credentials or certificates. A piece of paper does not a sound therapist make. Ask others for referrals, perhaps through a New Thought church, like Unity Ministries or Center for Spiritual Living churches in your area. More and more practitioners are popping up than ever before that are drawn to this important work.

Q: Are there certain bowls, instruments, or types of sound that are not good for the tender ears of animals?

Don: It's not about the bowl, it's about how it is played. When people ask what note of bowl they should get or what frequency, I say close your eyes and feel the sound and what feels right for you. Let your body, your intuition tell you. However, I have found animals resonate with the deeper sounds. Higher pitches seem to be irritating especially when banged loudly or suddenly. Regardless of either a bowl, flute, or drum, healing sound is never about the person playing the instruments, it's about the person receiving the sound. NEVER play any instrument or use a tuning fork close to the ears of any animal or human. The eardrums are very tender and can easily be damaged through unthoughtful sound.

All instruments are effective sound tools for animals; it's about how you do it. Two sticks tapping together in a low and steady rhythm creates a "heartbeat" that can reduce stress for humans and animals alike. You will find if the animal begins to move away or constantly watches you playing, then there is a mistrust of what will be happening. If they lay back and settle in then you know they are comfortable and receptive. Animals are extremely intuitive to sound, and they immediately tune into what feels right and what doesn't. Animals will instinctively be drawn to the healing modality that soothes their soul and raises their vibration.

Don Simmons with a horse "client" while facilitating a sound
journey at Chastain Horse Park in Atlanta, GA

◆ ◆ ◆

My hope is that you are now able to begin creating your own
sacred sounds for you and your animals, and will entertain
further engagement in opportunities to experience the healing benefits of a sound journey with a reputable practitioner.
Tune in to the *sound* of your own heart and birth a new level
of stillness and wellness within.

CRYSTAL THERAPY

I believe that crystals are far more powerful than we will possibly ever realize in our current lifetimes. Each type of crystal has safe and gentle healing properties and components that help us to align our energy within ourselves, our home, and the Earth. Earlier this year it was brought into my awareness that there was a healing center nearby that has a crystal healing bed permanently on site, and I decided to partake in a package of sessions. I was amazed to see and feel the energy associated with the crystals that were directly above each one of my chakras. Initially the healing sessions were quite intense, but as my energy and body consistently connected with and responded to the crystal's manner of healing, they softened and allowed a gentle alignment and healing to transpire.

My home is filled with many beautiful crystals that I love sharing space with and reaping the benefits of their energy. And I frequently have one or two in my hands while conducting remote healing sessions. Crystals bring us the grounding and connecting element of Earth energy that help us to feel safe and peaceful in this sometimes frenetic world.

Similar to sound therapy, animals will instinctively gravitate to the crystal that fulfills an energetic need they have. Over the years many clients have shared that they create crystal grids either inside their home or in their yards, and that their animals are attracted to lie beside them, sensing the benefit of their vibration.

Becoming familiar with how to use crystals and the healing properties they emit for yourself and your animals is a wonderful tool for your 5D tool bag! When I thought about an expert that I respect to bring you helpful information about crystals, only one name popped into my mind: Nicholas Pearson. I have two of his five incredible books on crystals (I highly recommend *Crystal Basics*), and they have proven to be my best resource of wisdom on crystal therapy. Nicholas has been immersed in all aspects of the mineral kingdom for more than twenty years! He began teaching crystal workshops in high school, and later he studied mineral science at college. He also worked for several years at the Gillespie Museum, home to the largest mineral collection in the southern United States. Nicholas is also a master teacher, sharing his wisdom about all types of crystals through presenting classes across the nation. And of course, he is also a huge animal lover and is very connected to the animal kingdom with his work.

Following are the questions I asked Nicholas about crystal therapy and his enlightening and useful responses.

INTERVIEW WITH NICHOLAS PEARSON

Q: How exactly does crystal healing work? How do/can they help us to reach and maintain a higher level of consciousness and vibration?

Nicholas: All things vibrate and generate electromagnetic fields, and those fields can be measured by both their amplitude and frequency. Using the analogy of a radio, frequency is the station and amplitude the volume. When two of these fields make contact with one another, the higher amplitude field tends to entrain or harmonize the lesser-amplitude field. Electromagnetic fields that are more organized generally have a higher amplitude, thus crystals are excellent tools for entraining the energy field. In other words, crystal healing works to bring more coherence or harmony into the electromagnetic fields around the body; as shifts on the subtle or energetic level take place, we also experience changes in mood and perception. This, in turn, results in changes to our pathology, as improving mood causes a chain reaction of chemical and electrical signals to course their way through the body. Crystals also have the ability to bring organization (or coherence) to our spiritual makeup. They are oscillators that transmit and receive energies; reflect, refract, and focus energies; store and retrieve energy and information; translate energy from one state to another; and amplify our intentions and energies for healing and spiritual growth. The more consciously and conscientiously we connect with the mineral kingdom the more crystalline we become, which enables us to attain and maintain higher levels of consciousness.

Q: What are a couple of ways for people to utilize crystals in their homes to expedite healing and growth for themselves and their animal companions?

Nicholas: Crystals can help us lift the consciousness of our home with ease, thereby benefiting all the residents—human or otherwise. Simple methods include gridding the home with minerals like clear or smoky quartz or black tourmaline in the corners of a room to cleanse and protect the space, as well as placing clusters of uplifting stones—such as amethyst, quartz, or celestite—throughout the home to lift and circulate the energy within. Crystal clusters also promote harmony among families and groups and help ensure a happy home. I think a big thing to remember when it comes to our animal companions is that they tend to reflect the emotional, mental, and spiritual states of their caretakers; thus, using crystals for your own well-being has a tangible influence on your animals. Work with stones that bring you peace, healing, and joy, and your animal companions will benefit from their influence, too.

Q: How should (or shouldn't) people use crystals during meditation to enhance their connection?

Nicholas: I believe that the most important aspect of working with crystals is to do so *intentionally* and *consciously*. So many crystal-lovers tuck a stone into their pocket and go about their days without any conscious connection to the stone itself. Crystals aren't a magic pill that solve all our problems. Be sure to cleanse crystals before use, and set the state for your meditations by focusing on your intention and envisioning that focus or goal filling your crystal—this is called *programming*. Cleansed and programmed crystals are better able to fulfill the goals we have in mind, as these processes instill a sense of relationship and cooperation with the mineral kingdom.

Generally, I think it's also good to remember to keep it simple at first. Work with just a small handful of crystals, one at a time, until you know them all very well. Spend time in quiet reflection with them, even if it isn't formal meditation, as this will help you build a better relationship with each stone. I enjoy a simple practice of contemplating a new stone in direct, natural light; I turn it every which way and engage my senses as fully as possible to really get to know it. In time, I try to create a perfect image of the stone in my mind. As my conscious mind is engaged in the visual and tactile experience of exploring a crystal, my subconscious mind is deepening its connection to the spirit or consciousness of the crystal.

Q: Are there any crystals that are too strong to have in the home with animals? Or are there specific crystals that they prefer?

Nicholas: While I don't believe in any firm rules for what is too much for anyone, animal or human or otherwise, I think balance is an important goal to strive toward. Currently there is a strong trend toward the "high vibration" or "high consciousness" stones like moldavite. I think some animal companions may be sensitive to these higher-energy stones unless there are also grounding stones present, too. Certain rocks and minerals have been associated with animals and animal communication in both modern and ancient lore. Some of those stones include dalmation stone, sodalite, many forms of jasper (especially mookaite), and serpentine. Always try to honor the needs of an individual animal companion when selecting stones for them, however. It's easy to project our own expectations and desires onto our beloved animals, so I often encourage clients and students to take a step back and work with crystals directly on/for themselves first before bringing them directly to animals. Giving animals the option to be around crystals or not is also important; animals should lead the process and have some sense of agency in their healing and spiritual journey. Some animals will feel entirely uninterested in crystals, while others may have strong attractions or aversions to them. One of my dearest friends has a Rottweiler who adores obsidian—she will go out of her way to hunt down chunks of it from the shelves to carry to her bed or chair.

Q: Do you also see the importance of their placement in the homes and the grids of communication between them?

Nicholas: I love this topic, and I think it is an important one to explore. The concept of crystal grids extends far beyond the beautiful arrays of stones in mandala-like configurations that we see everywhere on the internet. How we place crystals in our homes can, and usually does, create a larger grid. The best thing to do is to place our crystals around the home as intentionally as possible. This isn't always something we can do, particularly if our collections are too big to have on display all at once, but we can grid our favorite or most important pieces by placing them intentionally and strategically. No matter where our stones are placed, however, they are still within the Earth's electromagnetic field and are therefore still in communion with the stones within her body. The Earth herself is a living, breathing crystal grid. If we consider things from the big picture, all the rocks that constitute the planet— igneous, sedimentary, and metamorphic—are the sources for the crystals we work with in our practice (except for the rare ones of extraterrestrial origin). This means *all* rocks and minerals are interacting in some way as part of a larger system, part of a larger crystal grid. The network of rock and mineral that makes up our planet is the largest crystal grid that we have direct access to. There are crystals all around us in unexpected places, too: gypsum in our walls, copper that delivers electricity, and silicon wafers in electronics. Even living things are crystalline (there's a discussion of this in *Crystal Basics* on pages 20–25), which means that we, too, are part of the greater grid that permeates the planet. I haven't written anything about this phenomenon explicitly (yet)—although it is an idea that informs my practice.

When it comes to gridding the home, I think having a simple, intentional grid of similar crystals in the outer corners of the home is a simple way to set a foundational grid for all your other crystals to connect to. One important aspect of creating crystal grids is to connect or activate all the crystals in the grid. Grids draw their incredible power from the law of synergy and the principles of sacred geometry. Their synergistic effect means that their efficacy is not derived by merely adding the net energies of each crystal or gemstone involved; instead, they increase exponentially. Beautiful arrangements of crystals are also enhanced by the underlying geometries, forms, and proportions to tap into a deeper level of healing, spiritual growth, and planetary evolution. Consciously connecting each stone in a grid to one another and activating it for continuous work is also a vital step in creating harmonious and effective grids. This can be done by using a terminated crystal wand or point to trace the lines of connection among all the stones in the grid.

One of my crystal healing mentors, Samaya K. Aster (formerly known as Naisha Ahsian, coauthor of *The Book of Stones*) posits the idea that minerals of like geometries (those that belong to the same crystal system) create more harmonious and effective grids than those of differing crystal systems. She teaches methods to make use of a crystal's natural symmetry and geometrical principles to create effective grids. I sometimes use this approach, though I find that since all minerals exist

Nicholas Pearson with an "Earthkeeper Crystal"

within the body of Mother Earth they can work together in smaller grids, too. There's a lot of room for exploration here, too. My friends Marilyn and Thomas Twintreess talk about the crystal grid of the planet/cosmos in their third volume of the *Stones Alive!* series, and they have some brilliant insights.

◆ ◆ ◆

I highly suggest implementing the sage advice and guidance that Nicholas generously shared for yourself, your animals, and your home! It might be time to cleanse and program your crystals, and proactively engage with them in a loving and respectful relationship.

---※---

CLOSING THOUGHTS

It's your time to shine! You have been gifted a golden opportunity to apply the teachings of your animals by standing in the vulnerability and truth that resides in your heart. By utilizing the tools provided in these final chapters you can live more abundantly than ever before. You are on the path of the lightworker and your heightened level of consciousness is making a positive difference for all beings. You can choose to remain where you are or delve more deeply into your sacred purpose. Your path will organically unfold as you move forward with intention to become part of bringing more light to our planet. The place to begin is with your own heart, by learning to love and treat yourself as you do the animals in your life.

With unshakable certainty, know that you have partnered with the animal kingdom to usher in a new Earth that can collectively hold a fifth-dimensional frequency. Through our commitment to raising our consciousness and our vibration, we become part of creating divine harmony in our lives, our animals, and the world. There is divine potential within you that is awakening you to embrace the path of the wayshower.

Remember that, in any given moment, you are one thought, one breath, or one action step away from feeling connected to and reclaiming your power in the light of 5D consciousness.

Animals are our emissaries to 5D consciousness and will continue to drive humanity's evolutionary journey to create peace within their hearts. But now that you know you can choose to walk consciously alongside them, what will you do?

I hope you always find within yourself the knowing that you are worthy, you are forgiven, and you are so very lovable. Thank you for your respect and love for animals. Together we can bridge the gap to a gentler way of living, and create heaven right here on Earth.

Prayer of Thanks for Animals
by Tammy Billups

For providing unwavering support and service to humanity,
we give our thanks.
For revealing to our hearts the true meaning of unconditional love,
we give our thanks.
For the times we have been lifted in the darkest of hours
by a paw, a nuzzle, or slurp on the face,
we give our thanks.
For showing us the way to our hearts so we could make
a positive difference in the world,
we give our thanks.

Thank you, Divine Presence, for gifting us with the honor of
sharing our planet with animals, for when we look into their eyes,
we see you.

AFTERWORD

The Heart of a Wayshower

Around the globe, there are more people than ever before returning to the wisdom of their hearts and healing ancestral wounds for all who came before and for all who come after.

This is the path of a lightworker. *You* are a lightworker with a mission and purpose that is continually transforming and revealing itself. And you'll be pleased to know that you are already equipped with the wherewithal to shine your light even brighter.

You have awakened for a reason! Only the bravest of souls choose to incarnate on our planet, and your being here matters to its evolution. Your soul is nudging you to go beyond what the eyes can see, to have faith that there is a higher consciousness masterminding everything for the greater good. You are the alchemist of your own life, and never has there been a more opportune time to trust that the universe has your back and supports you in creating a meaningful life where you, like your animals, can feel the freedom of loving with your whole heart. Doing this, in and of itself, will raise the vibration of *all*. Our hearts fill with joy when we take responsibility for our spiritual lives and begin to love ourselves enough to reveal more of our inner light.

Wayshowers are lightworkers who choose to intentionally share their light and set an example for others to also walk the path of creating a new world grounded in harmony and equality. Each person's contribution is uniquely important. Some offer their gifts and talents in service to the masses. Others choose to focus on their own inner healing journey to enhance their vibrational level such that those around them feel lighter. The "right way" for you to become a wayshower is found in the whispers of your heart.

There is a radiant, luminous light in the center of your being that longs to be (re)discovered. Your magnificent animal companions are asserting that it is now safe for you to embrace your inner wayshower. The key is learning how to accept your unique and individualized Divine blueprint to become "authentically you" in the world. Then you will instinctively lean into creating and sharing your gifts and talents in ways that are welcomed and celebrated by your soul.

Begin the process by establishing a deeper relationship with your heart; it will promote an open exchange of energy and information with your Higher Self. You are sure to receive information overload when you go seeking advice elsewhere. But if you live through the eyes of your heart, you will feel everything with more intimacy and depth, and be guided by the treasure chest of wisdom held there. Our transformational evolutionary journeys are repeatedly pointing us to our hearts, to trust ourselves so we can become wayshowers. When we have peace in our hearts, we have clarity about next steps and we will act upon our internal nudging and spiritual guidance to benefit the greater good. Having meaning in your life is crucial to enhancing spiritual self-esteem.

You are meant to live a rewarding life that you love and actively participate in!

Here is my advice as you move forward to emulate your master teacher animals, embrace 5D living, and reveal your inner wayshower: Be kind and compassionate. Love yourself. Make 5D choices as often as possible. Be your own advocate. Create a life with inner spiritual security by strengthening your connection to the Divine and to Mother Earth. Let your tears flow! Keep your power in all big decisions. Trust yourself and your innate intuition. Allow the perfection of your life to naturally unfold as you birth the next generation of yourself. Try as best as you can to create a vibrational legacy complete with waves and wakes of positivity for all those that come behind you.

It is safe for you to breathe and surrender into the benevolent and protective flow of Divine light. And know that I will be championing your ascension process to the higher dimensions, to feeling more love and less struggle.

My wish is that the light within the hearts of *all* beings be stirred into awakening, to reveal to them the bliss of knowing their authentic selves and the honesty and purity of unconditional love.

Love to you and your big, beautiful, light-filled heart!

ACKNOWLEDGMENTS

My journey to write this book for you has been filled with many miraculous moments. One thing was certain from the very first paragraph: I was born to write this book. Though the idea seemingly "came out of nowhere," it is easy now to reflect and see that my soul always intended for its creation to flow from my heart to the pages of this book. And the good news is that I never felt like I was on this journey alone; I was supported and guided every step of the way.

First, I want to express thanks to the people and animals that courageously gave permission to share their animal love stories. Their ability to be vulnerable and reveal intimate details was courageous and honorable. Heartfelt gratitude to contributors Don Simmons and Nicholas Pearson for generously sharing their incredible wisdom in their areas of expertise.

I send an abundance of appreciation to Star Wolf for writing the wonderful foreword and sharing her amazing journey with Vision Wolf. In addition, I'm forever grateful to Star Wolf for connecting me with Jon Graham at Inner Traditions publishing many years ago. Inner Traditions has consistently been a wonderful partner, and I thank each and every person on their team. It is a pleasure to work with such a talented, professional, and conscious company!

Throughout the writing process I was surrounded by angels that I call friends who were more than willing to provide assistance in valuable ways that greatly enhanced the quality of the manuscript. Thank you to Helen Maxey, who didn't hesitate to say "yes" (yet again) when I asked her if she was up for reviewing the entire manuscript. As always, she provided constructive and beneficial feedback that greatly enriched the book. In addition, I send much gratitude to Judith Corvin-Blackburn for her big picture insights and advice on each chapter that enhanced the integrity of the book. Thank you to Tara Green, Diane Glynn, and Frank Maxey for their significant "catches" that I would surely have missed! And much appreciation to Paul Chen and Barbara Techel for their time to review certain chapters of the book that needed their special input.

The family "rocks" in my life are my sister, Shelley Westbay, and nephew, Chans Weber. I feel immensely blessed and grateful for their unwavering love and support in my life.

I never take for granted the sage teachings from my beloved animal companions, Bodhi and Rumi, in addition to the animal (and human) clients I am honored to work with each week. They are my best teachers, and what I learn from them is at the heart of each project I birth.

There were several nature animals that felt like representatives of the animal kingdom sent to support me on this project to keep me on course in their own unique way. Thank you to the hawk, golden finch, eastern phoebe, and bunny that boldly and repeatedly made their presence known at just the right times.

From the onset of writing the very first page, I felt the love and support of my spiritual team of advisors and animal council like a warm ray of golden light guiding my way. I am and always will be eternally grateful for their sacred presence in my life.

✳

Two incredible animal wayshowers have transitioned back to spirit since the initial writing of this book.

Rest in peace, Gamera the turtle
and Maverick the horse.

Thank you for sharing your sacred teachings
with so many.

Resources

BOOK RECOMMENDATIONS

Most of these authors also have 5D offerings and classes!
The first six were mentioned in this book.

Activating your 5D Frequency by Judith Corvin-Blackburn

Crystal Basics by Nicholas Pearson

Ho'oponopono by Ulrich Dupree

The Untethered Soul by Michael Singer

Waking Up in 5D by Maureen St. Germaine

Your Soul's Plan; Your Soul's Gifts; and *Your Soul's Love*
by Robert A. Schwartz

✴

Animal Speak and *Animal Wise* by Ted Andrews

Animal Talk and *Animals in Spirit* by Penelope Smith

Animal Spirit Guides and *Power Animals* by Steven Farmer

Bark, Neigh, Meow by Lynn McKenzie

Divine Beings; What the Elephant Knows; and *What the Owl Knows*
by Cara Gubbins

The Dream Dictionary by Jo Jean Boushahla
and Virginia Reidel-Geubtner

Dream Dictionary by Tony Crisp

The Five Personality Patterns by Steven Kessler

Hands of Light; Light Emerging; and *Core Light Healing*
by Barbara Ann Brennan

The Journey of Souls and *The Destiny of Souls*
by Michael Newton, Ph.D.

Sacred Geometry Oracle Deck by Francene Hart

Spirit of the Animals Oracle by Jody Bergsma

PRACTITIONER RESOURCES

Many of the participants who lovingly allowed their animals' story to be shared in the book are practitioners of animal communication, mindfulness, and healing. Their websites are listed below.

Andrea Montgomery,
animal communicator
montheart.com

Anielle Reid, author,
psychic-medium
magickandmediums.com

Anne Peek, tarot reader,
intuitive services
annepeek.com

Barbara Techel, author,
oracle card reader for
people and pets
joyfulpaws.com

Cheri Hayashi, animal
communicator, pet medium,
energy healer, spiritual intuitive
cherimichelle.com

Denise Olive, healing services
deniseolive.com

Donna Craig DVM, CHPV
outbackmobilevet.com

Don Simmons,
sacred sound shaman, visionary
consultant, speaker
donreedsimmons.com

Linda Star Wolf, shaman,
author, global educator
shamanicbreathwork.org

Marilyn Segal, life coach,
angel therapist
MarilynSegal.com

Maura A. Finn, healing services
www.finnevolutions.com

Michael M. Burke,
VST (vibrational sound therapist),
poet
michaelmurphyburke.com

Shalan Hill and Ann Pauley,
Posture Project:
yoga and massage
thepostureproject.com

Ruby Falconer, Astrologer
shamanicstarology.com

Sami Malcomb,
Founder of Wild:ness
wildness.one

ANIMAL HEALING
CERTIFICATION PROGRAMS

Advanced Animal
Communication Course
caragubbins.com/classes/

Animal Energy Certification
Training Program
https://lynnmckenzie.com/
animal-energy-certification/

Healing Touch for Animals
healingtouchforanimals.com

Tellington TTouch
ttouch.com

NO-KILL RESCUE ORGANIZATIONS I LOVE

Consider rescuing your next animal companion, or let it rescue you!

Advanced Animal Communication
Course
www.caragubbins.com/
classes/

Best Friends Animal Society
bestfriends.org

Good Mews Animal Foundation
goodmews.org

Helping Shepherds of Every Color
Rescue
helpingshepherdsofeverycolor
.com

Mostly Mutts
mostlymutts.org

Our Pals Place
ourpalsplace.org

Save The Horses
savethehorses.org

About the Author

Lorikay Photography

Tammy is a healer who walks her talk. Twenty-two years ago, she embarked on a deep inner healing journey after experiencing four losses within a few months' time. Through this difficult period, she suddenly had access to the spiritual "gifts" of seeing and sensing energy. Tammy is now a celebrated international holistic practitioner for humans and animals. She's a certified Interface Therapist (Bioenergetics), and healer to the healers. In addition, she's a pioneer and global educator on the many levels of animal-human relationships and has created experiential masterclass courses for those interested in learning more about the topics in her books. Moreover, she's the inventor of the groundbreaking, paradigm-shifting modality Tandem Healings, which accelerates the healing of humans and the animals with whom they share a soul bond.

Tammy's mission comes from her heart: to make the world a better place for all beings. She lives to see all beings be free, thriving, and forever joyful.

TAMMY'S OTHER PUBLICATIONS

Animal Soul Contracts

Revealing the higher purpose and soul mission behind our relationships with our animal companions, Tammy Billups explores the spiritual contracts that are created when a human bonds with an animal and shows how we come into each other's lives for a reason.

By discovering the soul agreements that underlie our animal partnerships, we can find meaning in the issues that arise with our animals and ourselves, support our souls' mutual evolution, and allow the soul contracts to weave their spiritual magic in the animal-human relationship. *Animal Soul Contracts* is a guide to discovering the spiritual agreements between our souls and those of our animal companions.

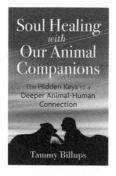

Soul Healing with Our Animal Companions

The animals we attract in our lives reflect us in many ways. Our connections with them run deeply, down to the soul level. Just like us, they are also on a journey to evolve their soul through their relationships and experiences, and each has deeply spiritual messages for us and intentions for our personal growth.

This book invites you to explore and deepen this profound relationship, showing how you can co-evolve along with your animal companions, experience unconditional love, and, ultimately, enact healing for both animal and caregiver.

Soul Healing with Our Animal Companions is an incredible handbook and guide to understanding the profound connection in animal/human relationships and its potential for mutual healing.

FREE GUIDED MEDITATIONS BY TAMMY

Tammy's free guided meditations offer listeners a way to dive deeply into healing specific emotional wounds and create a deeper foundation of self-love. In addition to being available on her YouTube channel, they are available on the free meditation app Insight Timer.

CONNECT WITH ME

Website—**tammybillups.com**
Facebook—**tammybillupshealer**
Instagram—**tammybillupshealer**
Youtube—**Tammy Billups**
LinkedIn—**Tammy Billups**

Index